PRESENTING:

ACTING AND DIRECTING

The Houghton Mifflin Communication Workshop

EDITORIAL ADVISER: *Kathleen M. Galvin*

Chairman, Speech Education Department
Northwestern University

Houghton Mifflin Company • Boston
Atlanta • Dallas • Geneva, Illinois • Hopewell, New Jersey • Palo Alto

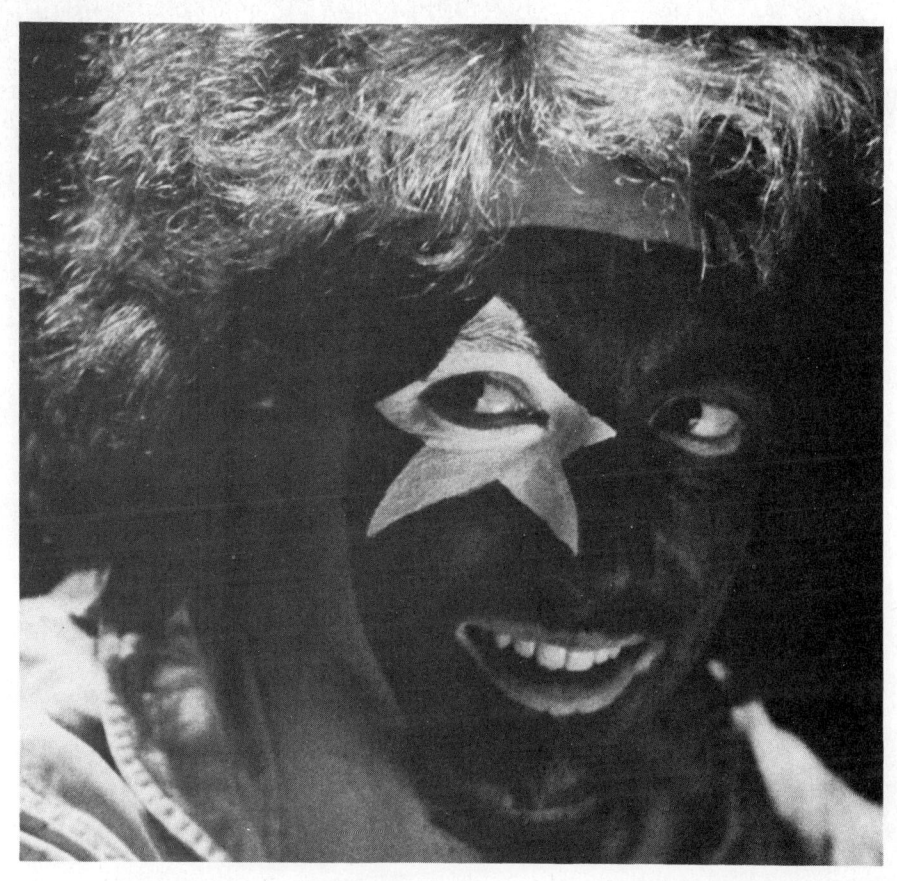

PRESENTING:
ACTING AND DIRECTING

Joseph L. Peluso • David Vosburgh

Copyright © 1975 by Houghton Mifflin Company. All rights reserved. No part of this work may be reproduced or transmitted in any form or by any means, electronic or mechanical, including photocopying and recording, or by any information storage or retrieval system, without permission in writing from the publisher. Printed in the United States of America.

Library of Congress Catalog Card Number: 74-17896
ISBN: 0-395-19761-9

PHOTOGRAPHS AND ILLUSTRATIONS

Page x (left to right), Bert Miller, Black Star; Jeff Albertson, Stock, Boston; p. 1, Bert Miller, Black Star; p. 3, Ivan Massar, Black Star; p. 4, Ken Heyman; p. 6, Evie Frost, Park School *(Peter Pan)*; p. 8, Owen Franken, Stock, Boston; p. 11, Stock, Boston; p. 15, Jonathan Goell; p. 18, Mark Haven (top photo); Dan McCoy, Black Star; p. 19, Owen Franken, Stock, Boston; p. 21, Mark Silber, Dimension, Inc.; p. 22, Bonnie D. Unsworth; p. 24, Donald Wright Patterson, Jr., Stock, Boston; p. 26, Rick Smolan, Stock, Boston; p. 32, Donald Dietz, Stock, Boston (top photo); Cary Wolinsky, Stock, Boston; p. 33, Stock, Boston; pp. 36-41, Ginger Brown; pp. 46-47, Jonathan Goell; p. 48, Doug Wilson, Black Star; p. 52, Rick Smolan, Stock, Boston; p. 53, Ted Spiegel, Black Star; p. 55, Ivan Massar, Black Star; p. 57, Chuck Isaacs, Dickinson College Staff Photographer, Carlisle, Pa.; p. 62, Jonathan Goell; p. 70, Stephen Potter, Stock, Boston; p. 72, Ellis Herwig, Stock, Boston; p. 77, Ken Heyman; p. 79, Jonathan Goell; p. 84, Ken Heyman; pp. 84-85, The Folger Shakespeare Library (corrected proof of *Anthony and Cleopatra* from the first folio of Shakespeare's plays); p. 86, Bill Grimes, Black Star; p. 90, Ginger Brown; p. 92, Jonathan Goell; pp. 94-96, Ginger Brown; p. 98, Hillberry Classic Theater, Wayne State University *(Julius Caesar)*; pp. 98-99, Mark Silber; p. 99, Bert Miller, Black Star; p. 100, Frank Siteman, Stock, Boston; p. 105, Loeb Drama Center, Harvard; p. 108, Ken Heyman; p. 111, Sean Clancy; p. 113, Peter Southwick, Stock, Boston; p. 116, Michael Dobo, Stock, Boston; p. 120, Vicki Lawrence, Stock, Boston; p. 122, Peter Karas; p. 123, Friedman Abeles *(Bye Bye Birdie)*; p. 124, Owen Franken, Stock, Boston; pp. 126-127, 129-130, Ginger Brown; p. 131, Ginger Brown, based on a drawing in *Scene Design and Stage Lighting*, by W. Oren Parker and Harvey K. Smith, used by permission of Holt, Rinehart & Winston; p. 132, Ginger Brown (drawings); San Jose State College Drama Department *(The Shewing Up of Blanco Posnet)*; p. 133 *(School for Scandal)*; pp. 134-135, Ginger Brown; p. 138, Kliegl Bros. (top photo); Donald Dietz; p. 139, Donald Dietz; Kliegl Bros. (last photo on right); p. 140, Donald Dietz (first photo); Kliegl Bros.; p. 141, from *Scene Design and Stage Lighting*, by W. Oren Parker and Harvey K. Smith, used by permission of Holt, Rinehart & Winston.

Cover created by Dorothy W. Moeller, using EPIC-II in collaboration with GTE Laboratories, Inc., Waltham, Mass. EPIC-II is one of the newest developments in the field of communication technology. It is an electronic device which enables an artist to change the shapes and colors of an image photographed by a TV camera and shown on a TV screen.

Title page photo by Rick Smolan.

CONTENTS

From the Authors   viii

1 SCRIPTS AND CASTING   1
How to choose the play and the players

2 CREATING YOUR OWN PLAYS   19
How to adapt and improvise

3 "ALL THE WORLD'S A STAGE..."   33
How to find a place to put on your play

4 ACTING, NATURALLY...   47
How to prepare to play a part

5 ACTING, LITERALLY...   71
How to work on a role

6	THE DIRECTOR'S ART How to prepare to direct a play	85
7	DIRECTORS AND ACTORS... IN REHEARSAL How to work toward opening night	99
8	THEATER TECHNOLOGY How *not* to be confused by production	123

Curtain Time	146
Books to Read	148
Glossary of Terms	151
Index	157

From the authors . . .

Move yourself back in time--back to when people roamed the wilderness searching for food and wore animal skins for clothes.

You live in a rough hut made of branches, and as you look at it tonight, you realize that you're going to have to cover it with skins soon because the leaves you use to keep the rain out have all withered and fallen off. But right now you're not going to let that worry you--tonight, you're going to the theater.

That's right. The theater.

The stage is in the middle of a small meadow, where the grass has been trampled down flat. The lighting is flickering fire; the costumes are deerskins with the heads left on; the actors are your tribe's hunters, and the script has never been written down and never will be. But to you the story is every bit as exciting as modern plays will be to their audiences in centuries to come. Maybe even more exciting, for you and your fellow tribespeople believe that performances like this have magical powers.

You lean forward as the first actor enters and prances, deerlike, around the fire. He is alone at first, but gradually other deerskin-clad people move into the light and dance with him until it looks as if a whole herd of deer is assembled. And you lean back and smile, knowing that the magic of this "play" will make the local deer herd prosper and produce. You will not be hungry this winter.

If you were lucky, you participated as an <u>actor</u>, or perhaps, as the person in charge of organizing the event --in effect, a <u>director</u>. Taking an active role--<u>doing</u> theater--is really the best way for you to be part of the excitement and the so-called magic of the theater. That's what this book is about--doing theater; but it also aims to give every reader a broader knowledge of theater as a whole. It is mostly about acting and directing (we've used the term "actor," by the way, to refer to both actor and actress), we have tried to show how you, as student actors and directors, can coordinate your arts and skills with those of playwrights, designers, and backstage technicians in working toward the ultimate goal of a production team: a performance for an audience.

The book is intended for everyone who is interested in theater. You can use it in a variety of situations: in dramatics clubs; in English, speech, or theater classes; or in mini-courses.

Theater can be anywhere and for everybody. We urge you to take part in it often and to sample the broad range of job assignments, backstage as well as onstage, which are necessary to the success of any group's production activities. We hope that the ideas, exercises, and activities in the following pages will help you to accept and enjoy the challenges of theater.

Joseph L. Peluso

David Vosburgh

SCRIPTS AND CASTING
How to choose the play and the players

What to put on. This question plagues Broadway producer and school drama group alike. Whether you are planning a major all-school production, a scene between yourself and one other student for acting class, or a one-act play as a dramatic club activity, the issue is—what to put on. Even if your all-school major productions are chosen by teachers, this chapter may give you ideas for plays and other dramatic presentations you can do on your own—in school or out.

There is no simple answer to the dilemma of what to put on, but to begin to find your way out, decide first what your reasons are for planning a performance in the first place. Is your group or class trying to raise money for some new stage equipment or a trip to a professional performance? Then you'll need to charge admission and do a sure-fire crowd pleaser—probably a comedy. Is your performance to commemorate a national holiday? Then find yourself a good historical drama or pageant. Perhaps your group just wants performance experience. In that case, several scenes from longer plays, chosen with an eye to each actor's needs and abilities, might be best. Maybe your group wants experience in self-expression and in working together creatively. Then you might decide to make up your own script, perhaps by developing a short story through improvisation or putting together a readers theater presentation. Maybe your English class is studying a story or novel that lends itself to dramatic production—try it as chamber theater, a readers theater form in which a narrator plays a central part (more on this later). Or maybe you simply want to learn more about theater. Then any kind of production will do, from the most complicated to the simplest, from Shakespeare to an action-packed children's play. It's up to you!

When you have clarified the reasons for your production, consider your resources. This means the place and equipment at your disposal, the amount of time you have to get the play ready, your financial capabilities, your audience, the season, and the actors from whom you will cast the play.

PLACE AND EQUIPMENT

Let's begin with your "theater." If you are planning to do your play in a classroom, then a full-length historical pageant is hardly the answer. Nor will you be able to show an intimate modern drama to best advantage on the football field. You may be able to pick a "theater" to fit your play (see Chapter 3), but if you already know where you *must* put on the play, you will have to find something that will fit the limitations of your playing space.

Consider your equipment. Some plays need a certain amount of furniture and other props, scenery, and costumes for an effective production. Does your drama group already have some of the needed items? Can they get them? What stage lighting equipment do you have? Lots of plays require only simple lighting—just enough so the audience can see what's going on. Other plays demand special effects which are possible only if you have many spotlights, floodlights, and a system of dimmers and switches for changing the lighting from bright to dim or from afternoon sunlight to twilight to pitch darkness.

TIME

Do you have only a few weeks before the performance D-Day? If you are going to celebrate Washington's Birthday with a play and it's already January 15, it's a good bet that you can get a one-act play in modern dress ready in that short a time—but not a three-act play set in 1776. On the other hand, if the school year has just started and you are planning for a late spring performance, you might even have time to do your own adaptation of *War and Peace*.

FINANCES

It can cost next to nothing to put on a performance—or a small fortune. Will you need money for building and painting scenery, for renting or making costumes, for printing tickets? If so, and if there's not much available, you had better pick a play that will be simple to produce. If you will be performing for a "free admission" audience in a classroom or an assembly hall there will be no revenue of any kind. Take this into consideration when you are looking over various theatrical "properties."

Does your group have money for royalties? A royalty is a fee paid to the author when a play is performed for an audience. Royalty fees range from five dollars to fifty dollars per performance of a nonmusical play; fees for musicals vary a great deal depending on your group and the particular show you select. You must make arrangements for all royalty

plays with the publisher or the author's agent. (You will find a statement to that effect, and instructions for paying, in the front of the published script of any royalty play.)

If there is no money available for royalties, then either create a work of your own or comb the library and play catalogs for plays in the public domain. United States and Canadian law permits a play to be copyrighted for a total of fifty-six years. After that, it is in the *public domain* and is free from royalty. Remember, though, that even a play that has no royalty will still cost you the price of the scripts.

Try as much as possible to look ahead to any costs that must be paid "up front," that is, before any money comes in from audience admissions. Some possible up-front costs to keep in mind: for scripts, costume rental or fabric, materials for making scenery (lumber, fabric, stage hardware, scene paints), props that have to be bought or rented, makeup, printed tickets, printed programs, promotion materials such as posters, flyers, and newspaper ads.

AUDIENCE

Of course you will keep your audience in mind when you are hunting for that right play. A play that would be entertaining to a group of teenagers might be a poor choice for an adult audience. Certain plays are better than others if you want to entertain little kids.

We all want to enjoy freedom from censorship. Audiences can be sensitive, though. Your best bet is to know the likes and dislikes, the tolerances and prejudices, of your potential playgoers. Your entire theater program is more apt to flourish if it has the support of your teachers, schoolmates, parents, and community. You'll be more apt to get that support if you avoid shocking them, and if you keep their tastes in mind.

SEASON

Your school's football season is in the fall; baseball season comes in the spring. Think of the entire school year as your theater season. You need to know what other productions are being planned. Find out what plays or types of plays have been selected by other groups in your school, nearby schools, and local community theaters. Three comedies in a row might be a bit much. A season that includes a comedy, a musical, and a serious play would go over much better. Your audience—and your actors too—look for variety in their theater experiences as well as in their lives. Give them a varied and balanced theater season!

ACTORS

Where will your actors come from? Are you limited to the members of your class or drama club or are you going to cast from the entire student body? Is there a nucleus of actors in your school with some previous experience on the stage? Must you recruit a lot of reluctant "extras" to play that army in the battle scenes—or will a small-cast play leave too many would-be performers doing props?

Try to use the actors you have to best possible advantage. An all-female cast for Shakespeare's *Macbeth*—or an all-male cast for *The Women* (by Clare Boothe Luce)—is probably not a good idea. Some directors disagree, however, and point to such famous performances as Sarah Bernhardt's Hamlet and Mary Martin's Peter Pan to prove their point. Regardless of how your group feels about unisex and opposite sex casting, you will have to be somewhat bound by the number of male and the number of female actors available to you—willing to be in the play. If you have seven girls and three boys who really want to perform, you should certainly try to find a play with seven female and three male characters. Keep in mind, though, that in many plays unnamed roles such

as "doctor" or "lawyer" can be portrayed effectively by either boys or girls. For example, in Ayn Rand's courtroom drama, *The Night of January 16th,* many of the smaller roles—jury members, for instance—have been played by members of either sex. Occasionally also, you will find a named role which, with small adjustments, can be played by a member of the opposite sex. In *The Man Who Came to Dinner* (by George S. Kaufman and Moss Hart) for example, the scientist Metz is usually played by a man, but it has been played just as effectively by a woman.

Another area in which you can be flexible is race. In recent years, the question of whether a black actor can play a white part or vice versa has been hotly argued in both professional and amateur circles. Some people feel that almost any play can be cast "color blind," with no regard for the race of the actors or the race indicated in the script. Others feel that actors playing married couples or members of the same family should be of the same race, but that there can be flexibility elsewhere.

A good guide may be, first of all, the playwright's intentions. A play like *Raisin in the Sun* (by Lorraine Hansberry) or *Porgy and Bess* (George Gershwin), both of which are specifically about the black experience, would probably not be true to the playwright's message if played with an all-white cast. But a play in which race is not an issue can probably be done with a cast of any racial composition or mixture.

A second guide might be whether the racial composition of the cast could be distracting to the audience: actors of different races playing a married couple, for example, when race is not an issue in the play. Try to analyze your situation—your actors and your audience—as realistically as possible. But try also to be flexible enough to avoid setting yourself unnecessary limitations.

Don't be afraid to experiment with the casting of the play as a whole. Excellent student performances of *Fourposter* (by Jan de Hartog), a play with a cast consisting of one married couple, has been done with a different pair of performers playing each of the six scenes. Twelve actors were involved instead of just two. The fascinating German drama about Henry VIII, *Royal Gambit* (by H. Gressierer), has been effectively produced with a different student actor playing Henry at each of the three main periods of his life. No one actor was overtaxed, and each could try himself in an exciting role. Remember, the happier the actors are with their assignments, the better their performances will be.

Don't be afraid, either, to do plays with characters who are older than your actors. Although there are plays whose characters are all or almost all in their teens, there is no need to limit yourselves to this kind of production—especially if you have some actors who can play "character parts"—old people, comic characters, witches, gnomes, or any other unusual roles.

If you are not sure how many potential actors you have or what their capabilities are—for example, if anyone in the school can try out for the play—you might want to hold some preliminary auditions before you decide exactly what play to put on. Then you can try to pick a play that seems to be within the ability range of your potential actors. These preliminary auditions can be approached in two ways:

1. Let each actor prepare a memorized piece, of his or her own choice. If the actor is working alone, this could be a monologue from a play or other piece of literature. If actors are working in pairs, it could be a short scene.

2. Invite anyone who is interested in acting to come to your audition, divide them into groups, and give each group an improvisation to work out (see Chapter 4 for ideas). Give them a time limit—about ten minutes. Then have each group perform its improvisation.

You may want to hear the actors again when you have decided on the play you want to produce—or you may even use the auditions of some of the better actors to form the basis of your play selection.

WHERE TO FIND PLAYS

Check the list on pages 43 and 44 for some suggestions for plays and scenes to perform or practice with. Standard play catalogs, such as those published by Baker's Plays, Dramatic Publishing Co., Dramatists Play Service, Inc., and Samuel French, Inc., are invaluable aids. They give a brief synopsis—plot outline—of each play and a breakdown of the number of male and female characters. They provide lists of royalty and nonroyalty plays, holiday plays, and plays appropriate for school use. And they tell you how to order the play you want and how much the scripts will cost. (See page 151 for information on how to order copies of play catalogs.)

Although catalogs are very useful for assembling a list of plays that might be suitable for your situation, only a reading of the complete play can tell you if it is really right for you—and if your group will like it well enough to want to put it on.

Another source of material is your school or public library. Some excellent plays published a number of years ago do not appear in current catalogs, but you can often find them in anthologies. Browse in the drama section of the library. Check the list of characters at the beginning of a play that appeals to you. Look at the descriptions of the settings, place, and time to make sure the play is feasible for your group.

☐ Go to the drama section of your school library or your local public library—consult the standard play catalogs too—and find the dramatic materials listed below. List them by title and author.
1. a three-act drama suitable for an all-girl cast of not more than ten characters
2. a comedy *scene* for two boys
3. a one-act play suitable for Hanukkah or Christmas
4. a children's play based on a fairy tale
5. a one-act play written after 1960, especially appropriate for high schools
6. a non-Shakespeare play which is in the public domain
7. a play that requires only one exterior (outdoor) setting

If a local author has written a play you like, don't be afraid to request permission to put it on. Or, if you have seen a television play or movie that seems to be just the right thing, write to the public relations director of the network or studio and ask (1) where you can get a copy of the script and (2) for permission to give it a local nonprofessional production. Sometimes a writer who has been unhappy with past productions of his or her plays has allowed schools and colleges to present them in a new light.

☐ Now you have some ideas about what to look for when picking a play. Using the following list of questions to guide you, choose a play you might want to produce during the current school year. Add any other questions you think would be helpful.
1. Is the play suitable for the occasion?
2. Do we have enough time to get it ready?
3. Do we have an adequate theater or alternate space in which to do the play?

4. Do we have the needed technical facilities (sets, props, lights, costumes)?
5. How much will it cost to put on the play? Can we afford it?
6. Will it interest and suit the audience?
7. Will it be a good addition to our theater season?
8. Do we have enough willing, talented actors?
9. Is it in good taste?
10. Will it be an interesting and challenging experience for our drama group?
11. Will it provide a worthwhile artistic—aesthetic—experience for everyone involved?

FINAL AUDITIONS

When your group has finally decided what to produce, you will probably want to have another set of auditions—tryouts—to make final decisions about who will play each part.

As with preliminary auditions, there are a couple of ways you can approach this. First, decide who is going to make the decisions—the director (if your production is to have one), the director plus some assistants, a faculty member, a specially appointed committee, or your entire group. Next, decide how to hold the auditions. One way is to choose scenes from the play that best illustrate the qualities of the leading characters. Perhaps the hero's personality comes through as strict and bossy when he speaks to his employees, but shy and tongue-tied in the presence of women. Or the heroine usually has a sweet, sophisticated manner of speaking, but becomes stiff and plays hard-to-get with her suitors in the early scenes of the play. Look for tryout scenes that give the actors a chance to show character qualities.

Choose dramatic scenes, emotional scenes, scenes with action, scenes the actors can get their teeth into. Find scenes in which the actors have to do something difficult you want to test—like laughing, crying, singing—scenes that require them to exhibit qualities like anger, conceit, kindness, nastiness, humility.

You may find a good scene in which many characters are involved. Then you can hear a group of actors read at the same time and have them

switch roles around several times in the course of the scene. Or you may prefer to have each actor read a two-character scene with a member of the casting group instead of with another actor. That will enable you to concentrate on individual actors one at a time.

You don't have to find a scene for every minor character in the play. Unless a particular role has some very special requirements that are best brought out by its own lines, you can probably get a good enough idea of an actor's suitability for a minor role from hearing him or her read other parts.

Improvisation is another approach to auditions. This is often a good method for actors who are inexperienced or who do not read well. (Some people who read poorly from a script give excellent performances once they have memorized their lines.) Call the interested actors together and, after assigning them parts from the play, tell them the basic situation of an important scene and have them act it out, using their own words. Switch the parts around until you have a good idea of who might be able to play which ones. Then, perhaps, hold a second (call-back) audition to which you invite only those people you think you might want to cast. At this point, ask them to read some actual scenes from the script.

Give your performers ample notice for the auditions—at least a week or ten days. Hold auditions on more than one day and at times that will conflict with as few other activities as possible. A sign-up sheet with the specific audition times would be helpful in giving you an idea beforehand which and how many actors are going to show up. You might also post (or have available at the tryouts) a breakdown of all the roles in the play. The breakdown should include a physical and psychological description of each character, as well as special requirements, such as singing, dancing, playing an instrument. Not all actors want long parts because of the extra rehearsal time involved, so it might be useful to indicate if each part is major, medium, or minor in length. It's a good idea to have copies of the script available in the library or another central location for anyone interested to skim through or read before the audition date.

At the actual audition, if it is a reading, have enough copies of the play on hand for each actor to have a chance to read through the scene he or she is to audition with. If you are using improvisations, it would probably be better not to have scripts available. Although some of the actors may already have read the play, they may feel more free to improvise if the scripts aren't nearby at the tryouts. You may want to give the actors a few ideas about the scene and the characters before they read. (If you have a supply of the character breakdown sheets handy, you will save a lot of time—and repeating for latecomers.) Talk with each person about his or her previous theater experience if you don't know it already and get acquainted a little before you start the reading. If a person has had experience in character parts, for example, or in comedy, you will have some idea of his or her suitability for particular roles.

The question of how to decide who is best for each role is a difficult one. The answer is often a mixture of opinion and fact, especially if you are casting by committee. People don't always agree on who is best for which role.

One of the most important decisions you will have to make before you hold auditions is whether you will cast only the best and physically most suitable for each role—or if you will cast for other reasons. If your goal is to achieve as polished a production as possible, then you should probably cast for "talent and type"—cast (1) those people who are the most talented and (2) those who "look the part" (you would not, under those circumstances, cast a slight, underweight actor for the part of a football star). If, however, your goal is to give actors experience, to learn more about theater, or simply to have fun, your casting standards can be a lot more flexible. You might decide to type-cast some characters (that football player, for example), to cast your most talented actors for the leads, and to cast minor roles on the basis of the actors' interest, cooperation, desire to learn, and need to express themselves or to work with other people.

It is hard, especially if you're not "type and talent" casting, to make up clear standards for evaluating actors at auditions, but here are some general guidelines. You may wish to modify them to suit your own purposes. (It may help at auditions to make copies of this or a similar list, and have each person doing the casting rate each actor. You can use the lists then as a basis for arriving at your decisions.)

PHYSICAL APPEARANCE
- Does the actor "look the part"?
- How does the actor fit physically with the people likely to be cast in roles of characters who will appear onstage with him or her (married couples, brothers, sisters, other family members, etc.)?
- Does the actor's way of moving seem natural? (This may be hard to judge in a reading, but you can always ask an actor to move around if necessary.)

VOCAL CHARACTERISTICS
- Can the actor be heard and understood clearly?
- Does the actor read lines intelligently, so they make sense?
- Is the actor's voice (or can it be) suitable for the part? (A child's voice, for example, is higher and lighter than an adult's; can the actor playing a child *sound* like a child?)

OVERALL EFFECTIVENESS
- Can the actor show emotion? (Was the actor convincingly angry, sad, loving, during the reading?)

- Does the actor seem to have stage presence? (Does the actor appear reasonably comfortable—assuming, of course, that he or she is no doubt nervous at the audition? Does the actor seem "at home" on the stage?)
- Can the actor take direction? (Can the actor follow instructions given by a director?)

This last point—the ability to take direction—is a crucial one. It is so crucial that it is a good idea to test it at the audition. Try to ask each auditioning actor to do something—move to a certain place or in a certain way; raise or lower his or her voice; be more or less angry, weepy, happy; read more slowly; move like an elderly person—whatever is appropriate for the part. If an actor shows that he or she absolutely cannot do what you ask, it will be wiser to consider someone else, or to cast that actor in a small rather than a large part.

Be sure that each person who auditions for you gives you a means of contacting him or her—homeroom number or home telephone number—so that you can easily notify those people you decide to cast. (You can post the final cast list on the bulletin board, too, but personal notification will cut down on the time needed to get a second choice if a role is refused.)

Make sure the people you are considering give you their class schedules and tell you about their regular after-school commitments—band practice, sports, jobs. Try to give them a tentative rehearsal schedule at the audition, too, so you can eliminate anyone immediately who won't be able to make rehearsals.

Remember that you don't have to make your casting decisions immediately. A call-back audition at which you hear only those actors who seem most suited to the roles is standard follow-up to first readings. A call-back is a necessity if you start with improvisations. After the first auditions, go over your checklist for each actor and line up several good possibilities for each role. Then have those people come back and read again. At this point, you might even want to consider a particular actor for an entirely different role from the one he or she read originally. Even after you have heard that person read a second time, you may want to have him or her read in combination with candidates for other roles to see how they look, react, and sound together before you make your final decision. It is important that your whole cast—especially those who will

be on the stage at the same time during the play—looks and functions well together.

One final warning. Don't let the choice of players become a popularity contest. Try to find the best possible actor for each role—or the actor who will profit most from playing it. Don't overlook someone who is not a football star or captain of the cheerleaders. The student who is most popular or the "person most likely to . . ." may also be the one most likely to bore your audience to death with a poor performance. The class cutup, who is terribly funny offstage, may freeze entirely in front of an audience. You've read all the right reasons for casting in this chapter. They're the ones to use!

SUMMING UP

Finding the right play to put on is the foundation of success for your drama group—so be guided by these important factors in your play selection:

1. The suitability of your theater space and equipment.
2. The time you have to get the production ready.
3. The money you have to cover costs of production.
4. The interests and tastes of your audience.
5. The theater season—will your selection add variety to the program of plays already planned?
6. The interests and talents of the available actors.

Finding the right cast to perform your play is a critical factor in the ultimate success of the production. Plan the auditioning and casting process with care.

1. Who will make the casting decisions (a single director, a committee, the entire drama group)?
2. How will actors be asked to display their talent at the auditions (by performing their own prepared monologues or scenes, by reading parts from the show being cast, by doing improvisations based on the selected play)?
3. What criteria will be used in deciding who is best for each role ("talent and type," actor interest, cooperativeness, desire to learn, need for self-expression, ability to take direction)?

Activities

☐ You are a student in a large public high school.
Your group has been asked to do a short play at a
Father's Night dinner to inspire the fathers to raise money
for books for the library.
a. Find an appropriate play.
b. Decide if you will "type and talent" cast or not.
Explain why.

c. Make up a casting sheet that includes the criteria a three-person casting committee could use for auditions.

☐ (This activity should be done only if your group actually plans to carry it out.) Your drama club wants the experience of touring a production. They decide to do a children's theater script (a published one) for the little kids in the local community. Divide into groups. Have each group take responsibility for completing one of the following investigations:
a. Find audiences in local elementary schools, community centers, playgrounds. Interview principals, teachers, leaders, and some children. Make a list of their past theater experiences, the kinds of plays they like and dislike, taboos or restrictions on play choice.
b. Check and list the availability and limitations of the physical facilities and equipment at the locations under consideration. What equipment would your group need to bring in? Can the location accommodate it?
c. Screen the plays and play synopses in your library and in standard catalogs that list children's plays. Make a list of tentative titles; cast breakdowns; requirements for sets, props, lighting, sound, costumes, makeup; cost of scripts and royalties. (Remember, royalties are often required even when admission to performances is free. Is the elementary school or community group willing to pay the royalty if there is one?)
d. Have a general meeting of all groups and coordinate your findings. Choose a number of plays to read thoroughly before you make your final decision. Make plans for auditions, rehearsals, and the touring schedule. Using the rest of this book as a guide, carry out your plans and do the play.

CREATING YOUR OWN PLAYS
How to adapt and improvise

Suppose you've checked out dozens of plays without finding one that your group agrees is exactly right. You may want to create your own script. You could adapt or improvise a nontheatrical piece of literature—a short story, for example—for the stage. Or you could bring an older play up to date and set it in the present, possibly adding a new dimension to it entirely.* The latter is a device that has been put to good use by respected dramatists of all periods. Eugene O'Neill's *Mourning Becomes Electra* was based on an ancient Greek tragedy by Aeschylus. *West Side Story* (by Arthur Laurents and Leonard Bernstein) is a modern-day *Romeo and Juliet* set in New York City.

---

* Be sure to check the copyright date of the story or play you want to adapt, and if it is not in the public domain, write to the publisher explaining what your group is and what you want to do.

19

In doing adaptations you can make whatever adjustments suit your needs in characters, setting, and even plot.

There are many approaches to adapting a play, a story, or any other literary form. Here are a couple that could get your group started. (These suggestions for adapting plays and short stories are based on group work, although of course people working alone or in two's can also do adaptations.)

ADAPTING A PLAY

Take an old, well-known play like Shakespeare's *Hamlet*. Read it. (Either have each member of the group read it alone, or assign parts and read it aloud with each other. As a group, discuss the characters and come up with a list of those you think are most essential (you may have to revise this list as you go along). If you were using *Hamlet,* you might decide on Hamlet, Horatio, Gertrude, the King, and Ophelia.

Discuss the plot and make a brief outline of its most essential events. In some cases (*Hamlet,* for instance) you might want to include things that happened before the play starts—you could begin your plot outline with the actual murder of Hamlet's father and go on from there.

Decide what time and place you want to put the play in. You might want to move *Hamlet* up to the present and set it in the heart of a big city—or on an isolated farm. You might want to move it back to fifth century Athens and add a "chorus," a group of people who comment on the action, like the ones used in ancient Greek plays. Or you might decide to leave it where it is and just do a simplified version.

If you want to do a simplified version, and you want to keep Shakespeare's language, break up your group into pairs and assign a portion of the original play—an act, perhaps—to each pair. Each pair then goes through its part of the play and picks out the essential lines and speeches (of course, using only those spoken by the characters that were chosen). Then get all the pairs together, assign parts, and read all the lines in order. Record your reading if you can, and play it back. Discuss your new play, make any changes you think would improve it, set a final version, and begin to rehearse.

If you want to put the play into your own words, assign or volunteer for parts and improvise the action according to your outline of the plot. In other words, get up on your feet and act it out, making up the lines and movements as you go along. One or two group members might play audience and offer comments when the improvisation is over. Keep reworking the improvisation until you are satisfied with it. Rotate parts until the characters fall into place. By the time you "set" the improvisation—make it final—you'll have cast your play and gone through preliminary rehearsals. (See Chapter 4 for more on improvisation.)

ADAPTING A SHORT STORY

Work as a group again. Find a story you like, preferably one with (a) several characters, (b) a lot of dialogue, (c) a lot of action. Assign parts and read the story aloud. (You can leave out everything that isn't dialogue.)

Discuss as a group whether you'll have to add any dialogue or any scenes. If, for example, the main character opens the story with a long description of traveling from Chicago to Minneapolis on a train and giving

up a seat to an old woman with whom he or she later has a significant conversation, you might want to consider acting out that scene as part of your play.

Then make a scenario. That is, list the scenes you want to act out and add a brief description of what happens in each. Discuss and change this until you're satisfied with it. At this point you will be ready to assign parts and improvise, as with the *Hamlet* project.

CHAMBER THEATER

Let's say you have decided to adapt a short story, but you find there isn't enough dialogue to carry the action. Pick someone to be the narrator, then, and have him or her read everything that isn't spoken as dialogue

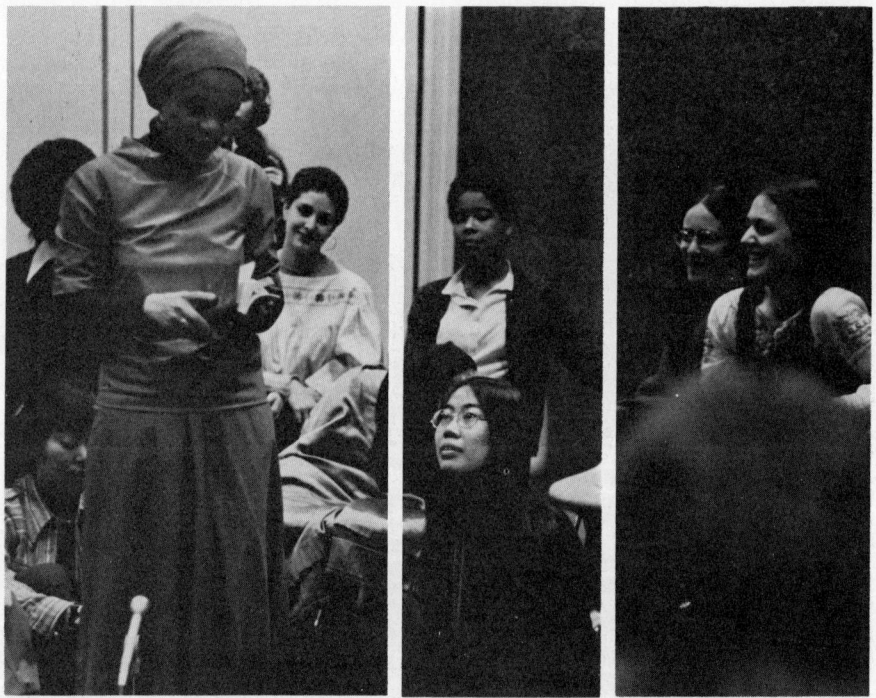

by one of the characters. Think of the narrator as the author of the story—the one person who knows everything about the characters, including their thoughts. The narrator can read any of the important "he saids" and "she saids" that contain descriptions ("she said, pushing the chair away"). He or she can also read all general descriptions given in the narrative ("It was a beautiful, sunny day. Susan got out of bed, walked across the floor, and opened the window") and can read characters' thoughts as the author described them.

In chamber theater, actors read their lines from their scripts while performing the essential actions. The narrator moves freely among them, reading to the audience as a storyteller might.

☐ Find a short story with a reasonable amount of dialogue—perhaps one you have read in English class and are familiar with.

☐ As a group, discuss and decide which lines should be read by the narrator and mark them clearly. Remember that the narrator may read anything you like—except directly quoted dialogue.

☐ Assign or volunteer for parts, including the part of the narrator.

☐ Books in hand, read through the story (record it if you can) and make any adjustments in the narrator's lines you think are necessary. (For example, you may find that a description of a character's feelings would be more effective if read by the character instead of the narrator.)

☐ When you have set the narrator's lines, get on your feet—books in hand—and read through the story. Actors should perform any action described; the narrator should move around freely among them (but stay out of their way). One or two members of the group might serve as directors at this point. They can watch the action, suggest changes, and solve any traffic problems that may occur.

☐ When the movements are comfortable and look appropriate, rehearse your story until it's polished enough

to perform. Then perhaps you can take it back into English
class and present it for other students. Discuss with your
audience whether the story seemed any different when
you performed it than it did when they read it, and
if it did, in what ways.

READERS THEATER

In readers theater, as the name suggests, the actors read from books or scripts instead of memorizing or improvising lines. They perform less action than in chamber theater; in most readers theater productions the actors remain seated on chairs or stools, getting up to move only when it is absolutely necessary or when movement is especially effective.

You can build a readers theater presentation around a theme, such as love or death, or around a particular author whose work you enjoy—or you can perform a regular play script as a reading. (Some plays have been written especially for readers theater—Dylan Thomas's *Under Milk Wood* is one of the most widely known.)

☐ Pick a theme—or pick an author.

☐ Each member of the group find and bring in several examples of literary works—poems, prose passages, fragments of letters, whatever—that either fit the theme or are representative of the author's work.

☐ Everyone in the group read all the material.

☐ Discuss how to arrange it, and decide who should read what. Pick one or two people to direct.

☐ Read through the material aloud and decide whether you should rearrange any of it, add more, discard some. Decide if some actors' parts should be interchanged.

☐ Read through the final arrangement of material. The director(s) should watch and listen carefully and, with the group, decide (a) if there should be any movement and if so, what; and (b) where each reader should look while he or she is reading—directly at the audience, at another reader, or beyond the audience. (Any of these choices is effective, but only someone watching—in this case the director(s)—can really tell which works best at any given moment.)

☐ Decide whether to add any effects, like music or lighting.

☐ Rehearse your production till you think it is ready to perform.

IMPROVISATION

You might want to create your production completely from ideas of your own, using improvisations and group creativity. Perhaps there is no script available that says exactly what you want to say about a topic such as drug abuse or war or marriage. Or maybe you don't want to be tied to a prearranged plot or lines that may not come naturally to you.

Then try improvising. As a group, work out a situation and dialogue from your own experiences and from your imagination—and build your improvisation into a play.

Here are some ideas for how to do improvisations—improvs, many actors call them.

1. Start from characters.

>an 80-year-old man with a limp
>a spoiled five-year-old girl
>the girl's mother, a rich young woman
>the girl's father, a playboy
>
>>OR
>
>a middle-aged couple
>their teenage son
>his girlfriend
>her sister
>
>>OR
>
>a young woman dying of cancer
>her mother
>her husband
>
>>OR

Some other group of characters who have some relationship to each other, and who could have some kind of conflict.

2. Put the characters in a place. You might put the first group in a railroad station, the second in a living room, the third in a hospital room.

3. Give each character an objective (something he or she wants). In the first scene, the 80-year-old man could want to sleep undisturbed on a waiting room bench. The five-year-old could want to have an ice-cream cone bought for her. Her rich young mother could want to convince her husband, the playboy, that he should not go away on a business trip. And the playboy father could want to get going because his trip isn't for business at all.

In the second scene, the teenage boy and his girlfriend could want to get married, his parents could want to talk them out of it, and the girl's sister could want to marry the boy herself. And in the last scene with the young woman dying of cancer—you decide!

4. Start improvising. Give yourselves a time limit—around five minutes—and start improvising, with each character acting out his or her objective.

5. Analyze. At the end of the time limit, stop and discuss whether the improvisation is going anywhere. (If it's really going well, though, keep on improvising till it falters.) Perhaps it is time to introduce a **complication**—

> either *from the inside:*
> In the first scene, the old man could get angry at the argument the parents are having and walk off to buy the little girl her ice-cream cone; the parents could think their child is being kidnapped.
>
> In the second scene, the sister could blurt out her feelings about the boy.
>
> In the third scene....
>
> Or *from the outside:*
> In the first scene, the playboy's boss could arrive and be surprised to see him—showing the wife that her husband isn't going on a business trip after all.
>
> In the second scene, the girlfriend's mother could arrive and announce that she is going to prevent any marriage between the couple because the boy's family isn't good enough or is of a different religion.

6. Feel your way. Sometimes a complication leads directly to an ending. Sometimes it doesn't—in which case, add more complications as needed. The original characters, however, should continue to play their objectives—to go after what they as characters want—until they win or lose—or until the improv, as sometimes happens, gets bogged down. If that happens, don't worry. Either start again with a new set of actors playing the same characters—or do a new improvisation.

Once you've done an improv with characters, place, and objectives already decided upon, you might try improvising from only a set of characters and see what happens. Or you could settle on characters and place only and then let the improv take its course.

On the other hand, you could go in the opposite direction and start from characters, place, objective, *and* a prearranged ending. This is sometimes helpful, because it gives everyone an overall objective. But it can also make your improvisation seem forced. If your prearranged ending turns out to be illogical or phony, change it!

You can also start an improv from an idea—a theme. Let's say you want to do an improvised play about pollution. You could start by having everyone in your group bring in something that he or she thinks says something about pollution—a photograph, a newspaper article, a poem, a song, an object. Have each person show his or her item and explain what it means. Then discuss how the materials could be put together to form a dramatic presentation. A song might provide background music to the reading of a poem. A photo might provide ideas for an improv to follow the song and poem. The object might be part of the improvisation. Another poem might tie the whole presentation together.

Or, if you start from a theme, you might want to make your theme into a statement:

War is _____.

Drugs are _____.

You could then add a character to your statement:

To John, war is _____.

To Susan, drugs are _____.

Add something more to the statement—something showing conflict:

To John, war is _____, but to his friend Harry it is _____.

To Susan, drugs are _____, but to her mother/brother/boyfriend/sister, they are _____.

Keep adding to the statement until you get enough of a situation to act out. In the first statement, for example, John might be a pacifist who believes war is wrong, but Harry might feel he should defend his country at all costs. War is declared—what then? Improvise and find out, adding characters and complications as you need them, until you have a beginning, middle, and end—in other words, until you have a complete play. Then you can set it, polish it, and perform it.

SUMMING UP

In choosing a play for your group to perform you need not be limited to already published scripts. You can revise the characters, setting, and theme of a short story or play to fit your individual needs and develop your own script. You can do a chamber theater production of a story or use readers theater to present a theme, a story, or even a play script. If you want to start entirely fresh, try improvising, starting with as many elements—characters, place, objectives, ending, theme—as your group can work with comfortably.

Activities

☐ Your theater class decides to improvise an original production dealing with a current social problem (pollution, ecology, child abuse, the generation gap, runaways, illegal drugs, welfare, housing, race relations, education, crime, etc.). Begin your project with a class discussion in which you determine:
a. the audience you want to reach
b. a target date for the performance—without one, there is a risk that foot-dragging will keep the production from ever gelling
c. the theme you wish to treat
d. whether the improvised play should be inspired by a piece of existing literature, a film, a song—or whether it should be developed from the collective ideas and imagination of the entire class

☐   Decide on characters and other elements, depending on the decision you made in discussing *d* above.

☐   As many of you as possible should improvise. Choose actors on the basis of their performances in the improvisations.

☐   Keep improvising until the group is satisfied with the way the production is developing.

☐   Set, polish, perform!

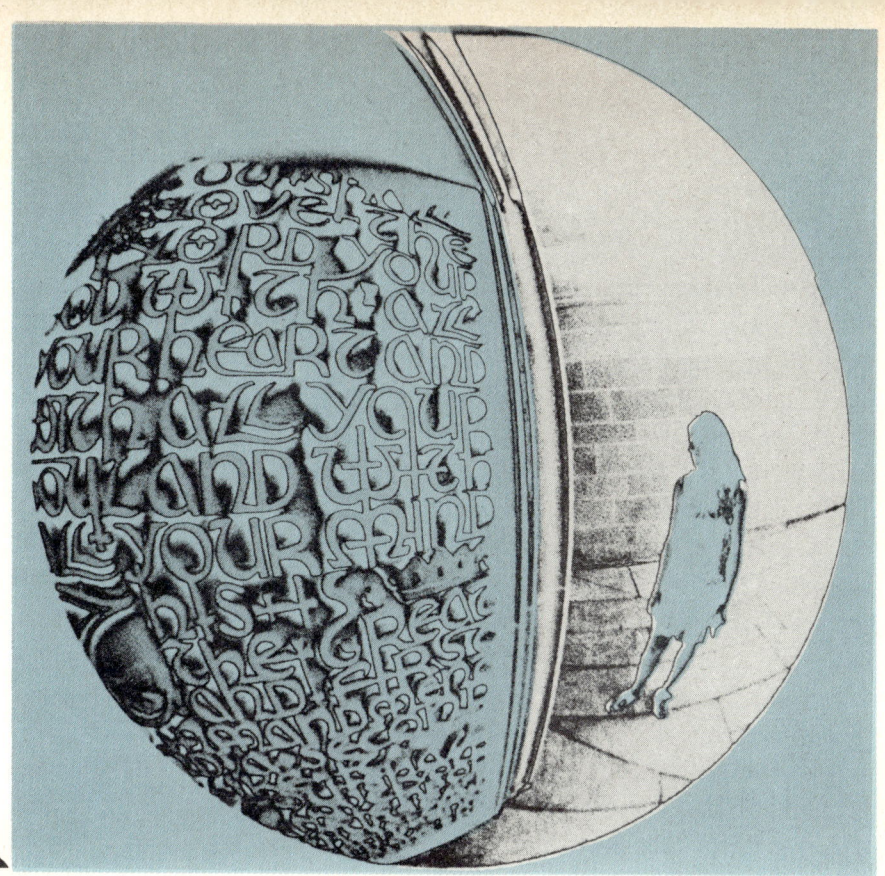

"ALL THE WORLD'S A STAGE..."
How to find a place to put on your play

Now that you and your group have decided what to produce and who to cast, the next question is, where you are going to perform? The most obvious answer is the school auditorium—but is that the *best* place? Before you ask permission to use it and start juggling schedules with all the other people making demands on its space and time, look at your production plans more closely.

It could be said that a theater is a "place to see." This takes in a lot of territory. In fact, it includes any place a group of people can gather to watch an event—from a classroom to a football field.

Two things should guide you in deciding where to present your play: (1) the physical demands of your production, and (2) the size and type of audience you expect.

Plays make specific physical demands. Some require a large acting area to accommodate complex settings and crowd scenes. Others, which need only modest acting space and a single, simple set, may be artistically effective only with a good, flexible lighting system that provides a wide range of lighting effects. If you want to protect the element of dramatic surprise, you might need a theater with a house curtain, so the stage crew can do its scene shifting "secretly." On the other hand, perhaps the play could be done under the noonday sun in the school courtyard with a few prop benches, and with actors *and* audience sitting on the ground.

Generally, you can't be sure how many spectators will come to your play—though if it's to be done as a school assembly program, you know you will have a "captive" audience of a more or less predictable size. But when you don't have that kind of guaranteed audience and must depend on patrons coming on a voluntary basis, you have to do some "guess-timating" about the amount of seating space to provide. You'd do well, too, to consider the type of audience that will be attending: a Saturday night dress-up crowd will probably want comfortable seating; a group of 100 primary school children will all want to be down front close to the action; your jeans-clad classmates would, at times, rather sit informally on benches, cushions, or the floor.

Most school plays are performed on conventional stages with the audience separated from the actors by distance and the proscenium arch (the frame that outlines the stage area and indicates the location of the invisible "fourth wall" through which the playgoers watch the action on the stage). A school auditorium is usually a comfortable place to seat an audience, and already established stages are usually more fully equipped than improvised stages are. But you may not always be able to use the auditorium, your audience may not be particular about comfort, your play may not demand fancy equipment—and it's even possible that your production might be more effective done someplace else.

PORTABLE THEATER

Theater is quite adaptable, as its history shows. It is almost as portable as radio, television, or the movies. You can create an elaborate production and offer it to a large audience. Or you can make a more modest, intimate production and play it to a small audience, perhaps repeating it several times so it can reach more people. You may even choose to

bring your play *to* the audience by making your production completely portable and performing it in other schools or for church and senior citizen groups. You could take it on tour from neighborhood to neighborhood, performing in playgrounds, parks, or wherever you can find both space and an audience. (Be careful to get permission from city officials or private property owners for outdoor performances—especially if you expect to draw a large crowd.)

You may be able to go on tour with your production within your own school, especially if you choose a play that is easy to produce and is related to other parts of the curriculum. For example, a simple dramatization of the cross-examination scene from Dickens's *A Tale of Two Cities* requires only two characters and a chair. It can be played effectively at the front of a classroom to history, English, or French students.

ADAPTING INDOOR AREAS

In a classroom equipped with movable desk/chair units, you may be able to get permission to rearrange the acting and audience areas. Then you can perform your play wherever in the room it will be most effective. You can do it as theater-in-the-round, with your audience surrounding the playing area. You can do it . . .

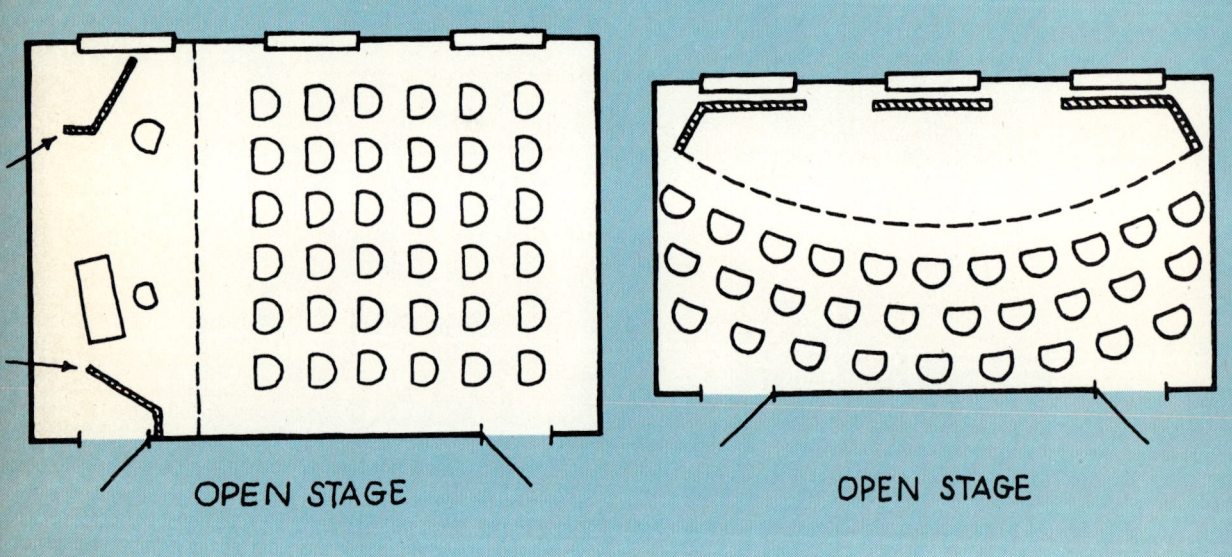

OPEN STAGE

OPEN STAGE

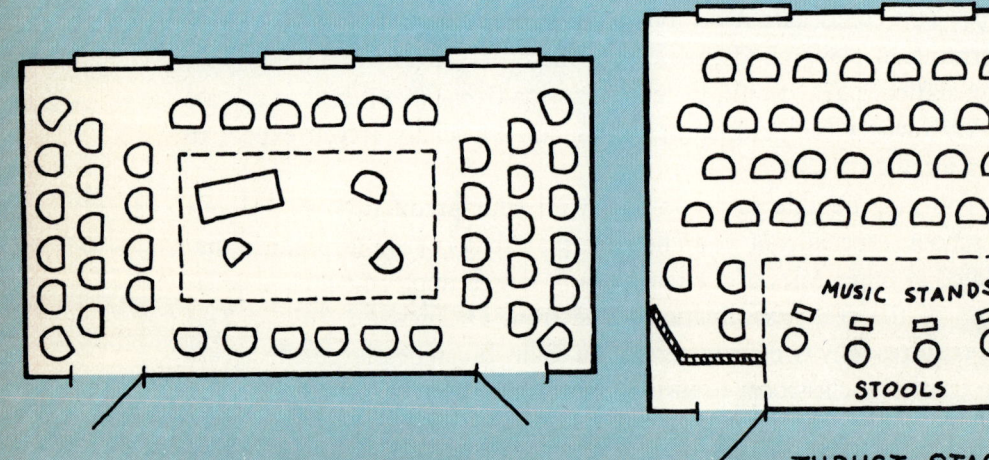

THEATER-IN-THE-ROUND
(ARENA STAGE)

THRUST STAGE
SET UP FOR READERS THEATER

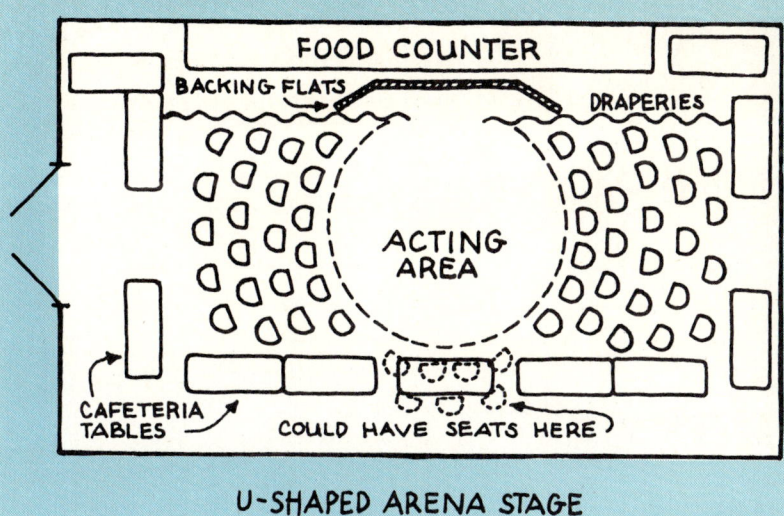

U-SHAPED ARENA STAGE

If you need a large space but don't want to use the auditorium, how about asking if you can use the cafeteria or gymnasium?

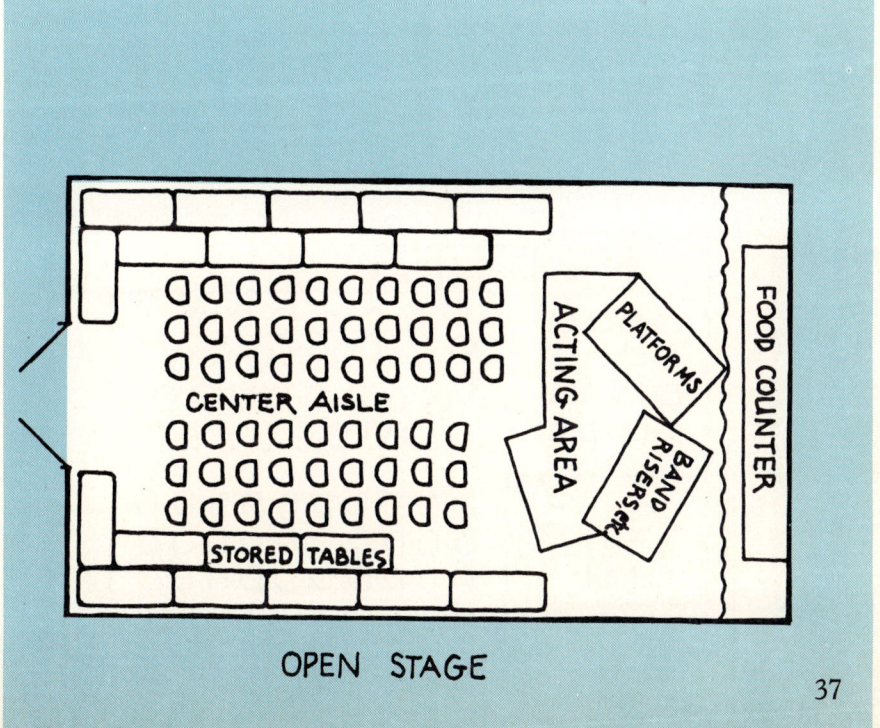

OPEN STAGE

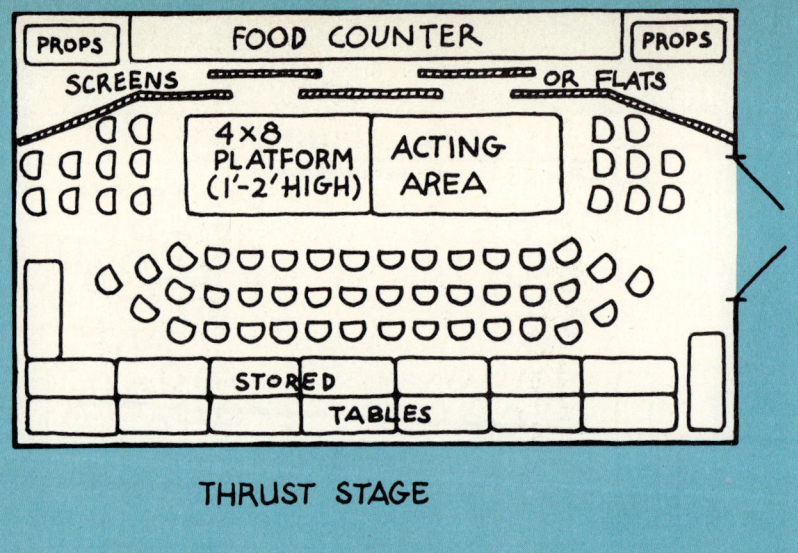

THRUST STAGE

A cafeteria provides an open working space with completely flexible seating. You might bring in some platforms (risers)—borrow the ones the school band uses to raise the musicians in the back so that they are higher than the ones in the front—and use them to elevate all or a portion of either your "stage" or the audience, to insure that everyone can see what's going on. You could use some of the cafeteria furniture as props (you might want to drape it with fabric so that it won't remind your audience too much of lunch period). If you're not using the entire room, you might outline the audience section with cafeteria tables to give your viewers a more intimate feeling.

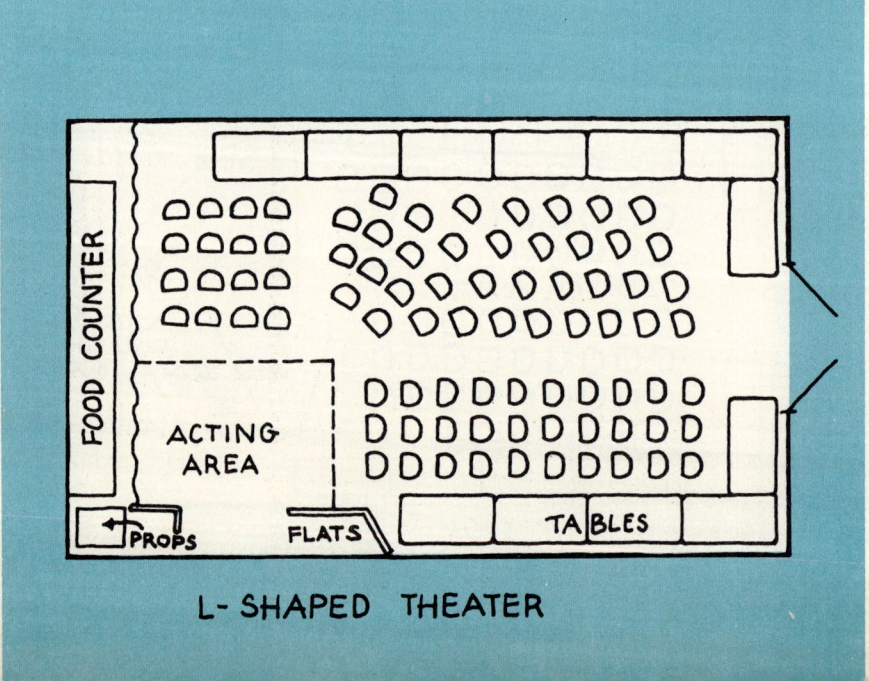

L-SHAPED THEATER

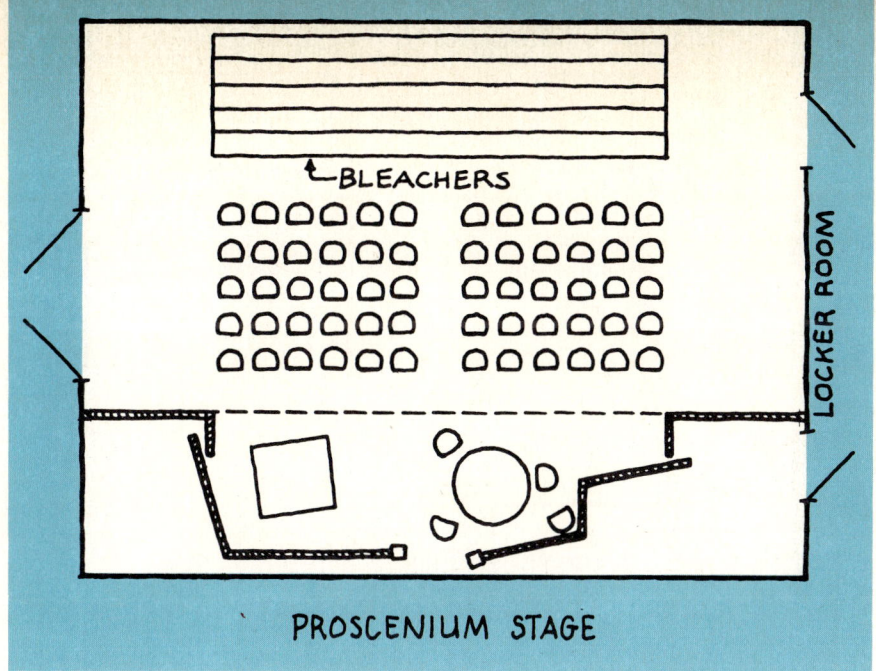

PROSCENIUM STAGE

The gymnasium, if it has a built-in bleacher section, may already present you with a raised seating area. But, more important, it will give you almost unlimited open space and height in which to construct your playing area. You are free to create any type of stage: thrust stage—with the audience sitting on three sides of the raised acting area; arena stage—with the audience surrounding the action; or a flexible stage with audience seating possible in an endless variety of arrangements (L-shaped, U-shaped, railroad-track shaped). The diagrams will give you an idea of how a gym can be used for different kinds of staging.

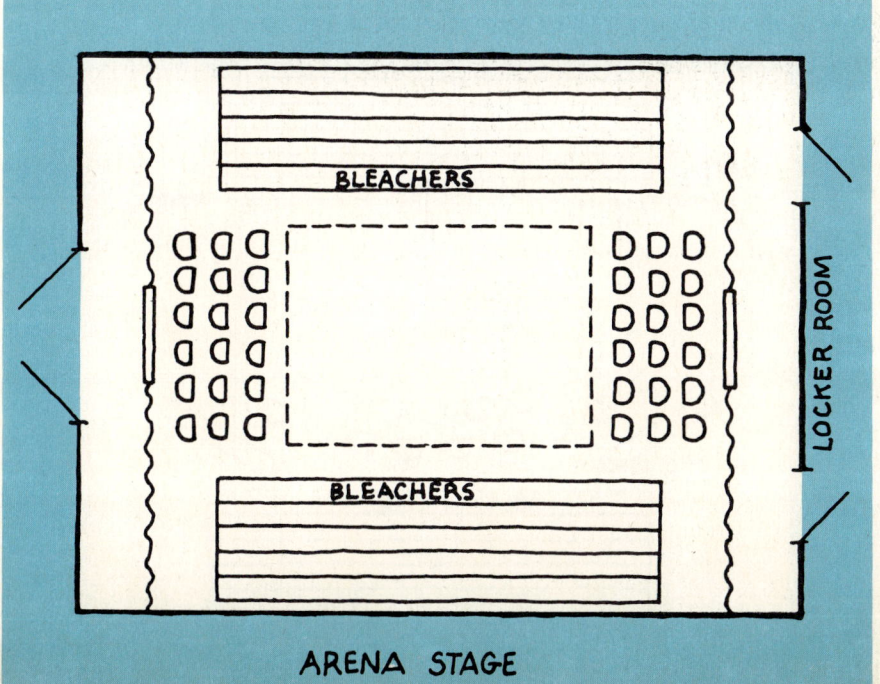

ARENA STAGE

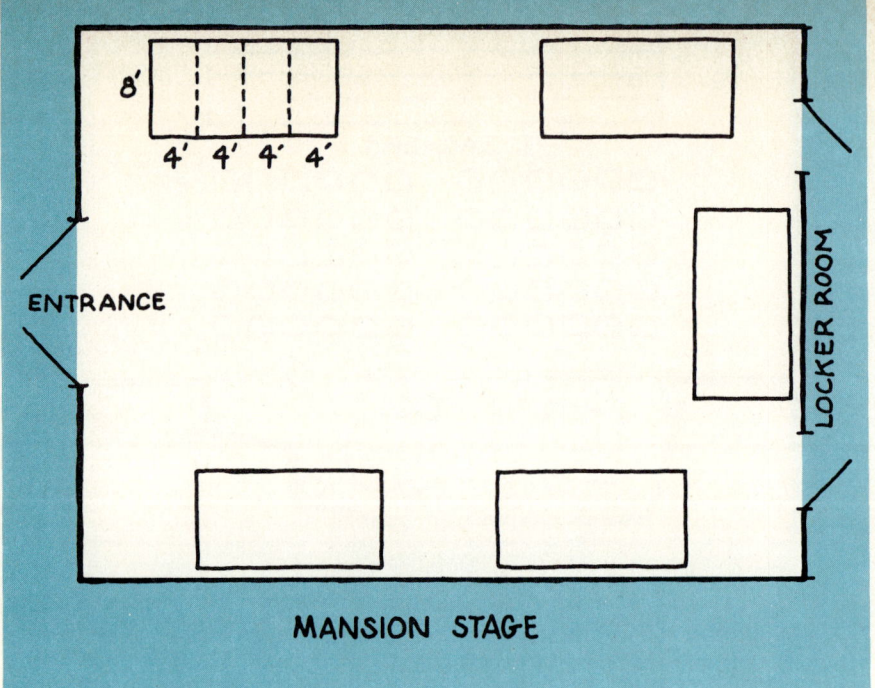

MANSION STAGE

You may even elect to use the gym for the construction of a number of stages something like the "mansions" used in Medieval days. These were compact stages (representing, for example, heaven, Herod's palace, the temple, hell) built in various locations in a church, around a village square, or side-by-side atop a single raised platform.

Your audience could follow the scenes and the action of the play by moving from one area to another in much the same way that spectators move from stage to stage in a circus side-show.

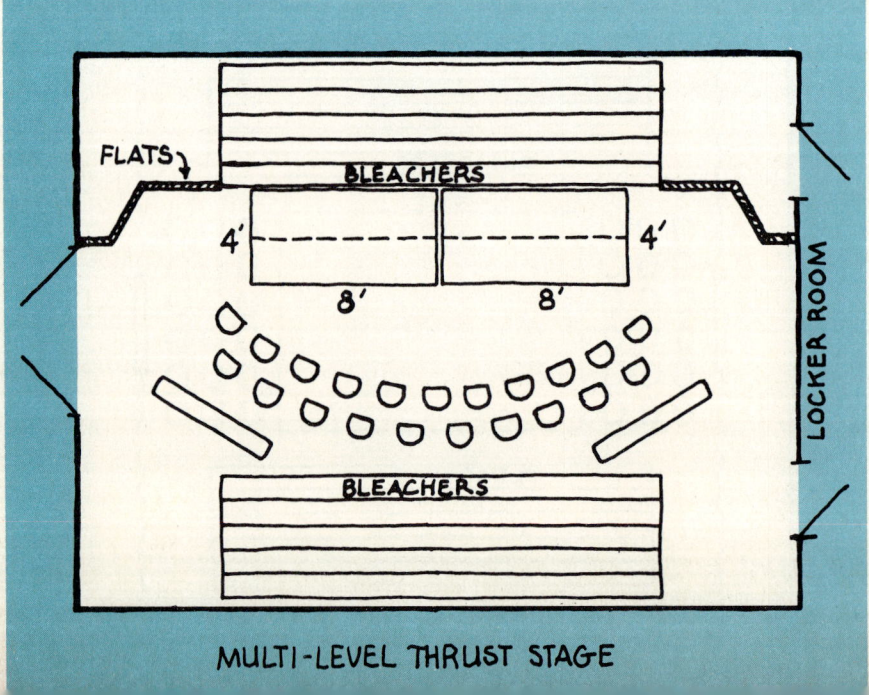

MULTI-LEVEL THRUST STAGE

If, however, you wish to or must use the auditorium for your production, you still need not be bound by the confines of the proscenium arch. Think of the whole auditorium as your playing area if you want to bridge the gap between performer and viewer and bring the audience into a more personal relationship with the action. Try an "extended proscenium" production; that is, mentally relocate the proscenium arch and set the action of the play in any part of the auditorium you want. Extend the stage out into the "house"—the audience area. Use any steps or balconies already in the room; add platforms along the house walls to create side stages or even completely separate playing areas. Plan to have some actors enter down the center aisle, or even play a short scene there.

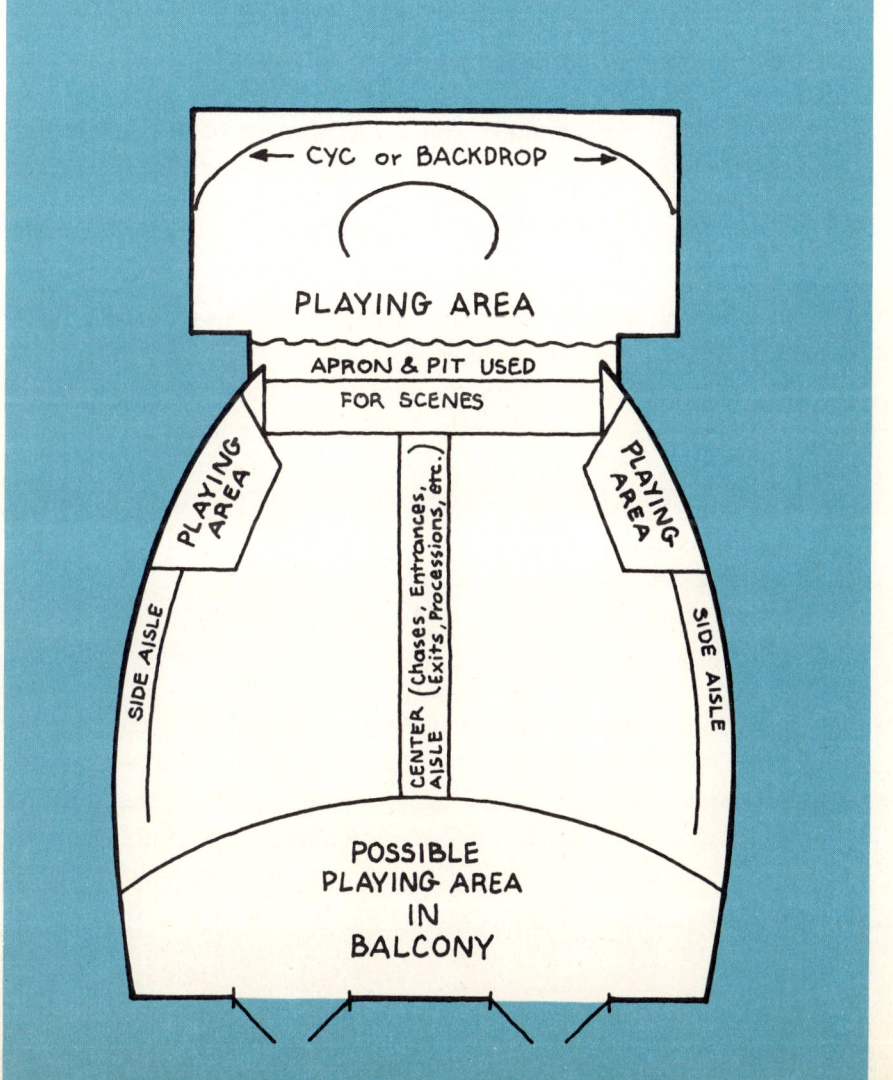

USING THE OUTDOORS

Of course you could be planning a large-scale production that requires extensive space and a "cast of thousands" and for which a bird's eye view would be an advantage for the spectator. Historical pageants, large-cast musicals (maybe *The Music Man*, by M. Willson, complete with the full school marching band) or Shakespeare's *Julius Caesar*—mob scenes and all—might go over well in a very large, open space. Consider the football field or some other outdoor location.

Stadiums and athletic fields with bleachers, because of their built-in seating, are good places for large outdoor productions. So are fields, especially if there is a corner backed with bushes to play against. Steps are terrific, especially for Greek plays and Shakespeare. They can accomodate large groups of actors, and their many levels offer lots of possibilities for acting areas.

Consider staging an outdoor production using "pageant cars" (rolling stages) like the ones that were so popular in Medieval England. Each scene would be mounted—complete with scenery and actors—on a separate wagon and rolled in front of the audience. At the end of the scene that wagon would be rolled away and the next one would take its place. It would be very dramatic to use them if you're from a part of the country where farm wagons are easy to come by.

There is a problem, though, with outdoor theaters: sound. Without some kind of sound system, human voices tend to get lost in the open air, especially in a totally unenclosed area like a field.

The first thing you should do when you've selected an outdoor playing area, then, is to test it for sound. Your test won't be entirely accurate, because the presence of an audience affects the acoustics (the actors' voices will to some extent both "bounce off" and be absorbed by the people in the audience). But you can get some idea of the acoustics by getting everyone in your group together in the playing area and having them read their lines while someone walks around the audience area listening. This person finds out if the actors can be heard and if so, which parts of the proposed seating area seem to be easiest to hear from. If the situation seems hopeless, you might want to use microphones and a public address system—or move back indoors. If live intimate dialogue isn't crucial to your production, you can even record your lines on tape and broadcast them through the public address system while the performers pantomime the action. This technique is used extensively by such large touring extravaganzas as circuses, ice shows, and "Disney-on-Parade."

☐ From the following list of plays, select:
1. one that could be satisfactorily produced in a classroom, and
2. one that could be satisfactorily produced in a nonclassroom space or area of your school (not including your school auditorium or theater).

(Of course, to make an intelligent choice, you will have to consult the synopses of the plays in play catalogs or the information and descriptions which are included in actual playscripts.)

☐ Make a diagram showing where you would locate the audience section and the acting area. Explain why your play would be suitable for performance in the area you chose.

The Boor, by Anton Chekov
The Devil and Daniel Webster, by Stephen Vincent Benét
The Happy Journey to Trenton and Camden, by Thornton Wilder
The High School, adapted by Arnold Perl (from *The World of Sholom Aleichem* by Maurice Samuel)
In the Zone, by Eugene O'Neill
Lawyer Lincoln, by C. Webb and B. Smith
The Long Christmas Dinner, by Thornton Wilder
The Man in the Bowler Hat, by A. A. Milne
A Marriage Proposal, by Anton Chekov
A Midsummer Night's Dream, by William Shakespeare
Our Town, by Thornton Wilder
The People, Yes, by Carl Sandburg
A Raisin in the Sun, by Lorraine Hansberry
The Red Velvet Coat, by Josephina Niggli
Romeo and Juliet, by William Shakespeare

The Servant of Two Masters, by Carlo Goldoni
Sorry Wrong Number, by Lucille Fletcher
Subway Circus, by William Saroyan
Sunday Costs Five Pesos, by Josephina Niggli
To Be Young, Gifted and Black, by Lorraine Hansberry
Under Milk Wood, by Dylan Thomas
The World of Carl Sandburg, by Norman Corwin
You're a Good Man, Charlie Brown, by Clark Gesner

Let the only rein on your imagination be this—that nothing you decide to do is for the sake of novelty only. Your purpose is to increase the audience's understanding and enjoyment of your presentation. Everything in your production must further this goal—nothing must detract from it.

SUMMING UP

If you can get one person to stand still long enough to hear you perform Mark Antony's "Friends, Romans, countrymen..." speech from *Julius Caesar,* you've found a theater. A makeshift one, admittedly—but a theater nonetheless. Whatever theater you choose must suit the physical requirements of the play; it must be large enough to hold your audience, and designed so that they can see and hear well, and it should be reasonably comfortable.

Most of your plays are probably produced in the school auditorium, which in most cases features a conventional stage framed by a proscenium arch. But you have countless possibilities for improvising theaters in your school's classrooms, lecture and study halls, cafeteria, gymnasium, outside steps, courtyard, lawn, tennis courts or football stadium.

Your play might be most effective in an audience-and-stage arrangement different from that in a traditional proscenium theater. Consider doing shows on "homemade" thrust, arena, or extended proscenium stages, on wagons, or in environments where the audience section is L-shaped, U-shaped, square, circular, or railroad-track-shaped.

Remember! Pick your theater and staging style to give you the best chance of getting the playwright's message across to the audience.

Activities

☐   Do an inventory of all the areas in your school building and on your school grounds (excluding the auditorium) that would be suitable for putting on plays. (Working in small groups might be easiest.) For each space you find suitable, record the following information on a large index card:

```
              Workable Areas for Staging Productions
   The Space: _____
   Location: _____
   Stage Possibilities          Possible Dimensions
   (arena, thrust, etc.)        of Acting Area
   _____         _____
   _____         _____
   Possible Audience Set-up     Seating Capacity
   (U-shaped, L-shaped, etc.)
   _____         _____
   _____         _____

   Types of Plays for which suitable: _____
   _____
   Particular Advantages of Space: _____
   _____
   Limitations of Space: _____
   _____
```

Compare notes with other groups, make a single master file, and keep it for future reference.

☐   Divide half the class into groups of three to five persons. Each group select a short scene and prepare it (you don't need to memorize it; you can read it or improvise it if you want) for presentation in an improvised "theater." Use any other space you wish (except the auditorium) inside the school building or on the school grounds. Invite the class to see your show. Follow the performance with a discussion on the question, "In what ways was the production enriched because of this particular 'theater'?"

☐   Divide the remaining half of the class into groups of three to five persons. Each group select a short scene and prepare it for presentation (again, memorizing is optional) in the school auditorium. Don't use the stage proper, however; use the extended proscenium method of staging. As above, perform for the class and discuss the suitability of the theater space to the scene.

ACTING, NATURALLY...
How to prepare to play a part

What was the last good television production you saw? Whatever it was, you can be sure that a well-coordinated team of writer, director, designers, technicians, and actors worked many hours to produce it, and that in addition they worked for many years beforehand to master their particular arts and crafts. The artists of the live theater, too, labor for years learning their craft—and usually work for many weeks to prepare each show they do.

FREEING THE ACTOR'S INSTRUMENTS

All artists use instruments: the Rolling Stones use strings and percussion; Michelangelo worked with brushes and chisels; New York subway graffiti artists Rico III and Snake 1 wield magic markers and cans of spray paint.

The actor, however, has a different kind of instrument: his or her own voice and body. Even more important, however, are the actor's inner resources: *intellect, memory, imagination, emotion,* and *senses.* Think of basic training in acting as a process that combines rediscovery of everything you ever observed, thought, accomplished, and imagined with discovery of ways to make your voice and body as flexible and responsive as they can possibly be. The ultimate goal is to free all your physical, mental, and emotional resources to the point where you can deal fully with the dialogue and characterization demands of any part you play.

That may sound like a lot, but it's really not impossible if you take it one step at a time. You can start with:

Relaxation

If you are playing an old person and your muscles are so tense that you're uncomfortable when you try to walk with a slow, shuffling gait, you'll probably end up returning to your normal way of walking halfway through the performance. That way you'll avoid the discomfort—but your characterization will suffer. If your body is free of tension, however, it won't fight back when you ask it to express a character for you. There are some simple techniques you can use to help you relax.

Recognize your specific tensions — First, check to feel where your tensions are: In your face? (Do you often frown, squint, purse your lips, clench your teeth?) In your hands? (Do you often clench your fists, snap

or tap your fingers, pick at your cuticles or fingernails?) In your back? (Do you often "freeze" your backbone, shrug your shoulders, rest your top weight heavily on the small of your back?) In your legs and feet? (Do you often crinkle your toes, tap your feet, stand stiff-legged and lock-kneed?) Then RELAX!

- [ ] Drop your chin and open your mouth wide in a big but easy yawn; dangle, bob and rotate your head.

- [ ] Shake and "waggle" your hands and fingers vigorously but loosely at the wrists.

- [ ] Rotate the upper part of your body at the waist; rotate your shoulders in their sockets.

- [ ] Swing your legs—one at a time, of course—back and forth, bending them at the knee and the ankle (it may help to hold onto a chair); wiggle your toes free from their crouched position within your shoes.

The next time you're rushing to the cafeteria, concentrate on using only those muscles of your legs and feet that are *absolutely necessary* to propel you to the head of the lunch line. Do the same when you are riding a bike, walking, sitting. When you take part in sports and other activities that require physical exertion, check from time to time to make sure that you are using only those muscles required. If you are, that's a pretty good sign that the rest of your body is relaxed.

Involve yourself with the role — Perhaps the main cause of tension for the beginning actor during rehearsal and performance is the audience. What will the audience think of my characterization? What will the audience think of *me*? Nothing can be more self-defeating. It is difficult, if not impossible, to do two things at one time—to play a role and worry about the audience. Forget about the audience and concentrate on the character and the situation. Believe that what you are performing is real! When you succeed in focusing all your attention on the scene, you'll become so involved that you will probably be able to forget both the audience and your own tensions. And when you've done that, you'll have a much better chance of playing your part well (and pleasing the audience).

Here is another exercise in relaxation. It will also give you a chance to do a little acting—and see how it feels to become involved in a role.

☐ Imagine that your classroom is the interior of a bank in the old West and you and your classmates—all but one—are tellers, guards, clerks, and customers going about their routine business. The remaining student is an armed, masked "desperado."

☐ Suddenly, the desperado enters and barks: "Reach high! This is a stickup!"

☐ You, and every other customer, clerk, or whoever, take a large, deep breath and stretch your hands, arms, and body as high as you can. React with appropriate dismay, shock, fear, etc.

☐ After five or six seconds, the desperado unmasks, lowers his or her weapon—partially—and proclaims: "I was only kidding. Relax!"

☐ Suspicious, the rest of you begin *slowly* to exhale and relax, starting with the tips of your fingers, then your palms, wrists, elbows, shoulders, all the muscles of your face, neck, back, waist, thighs, knees, calves, ankles, and toes.

☐ When you are free of all tension, take another full breath, then release it with a long sigh of relief.

Concentration

Concentration, as we have said, is a good tension-easer. But it is also essential to convincing performances. But *where* should you concentrate? On the audience? On your body? Your voice? Absolutely not! Concentrate on the play and on your character. A young actress in a summer theater who had been told once too often to concentrate on her character decided to see what would happen if she purposely concentrated on something outside the play. In rehearsal, she let her eyes scan the exit lights, the director and stage manager sitting in the fourth row, a sweater someone had left on the floor of the theater. At the same time, she tried to say her lines and participate in the scene. The result: chaos! Not only did she forget her lines, she also found, after only a few seconds, that she had no idea of what was going on in the scene. She quickly shifted her concentration back and luckily was able to recapture it before the scene fell apart.

☐ Pair off. While your partner performs a series of simple actions—waving, stretching, scratching—imagine that you are a mirror and reflect every action. Concentrate on every facial expression, gesture, and physical attitude. Copy everything your partner does.

☐ Reverse roles with your partner and repeat the exercise.

☐ When you have done the exercise a few times with different partners, pair off again. This time the pairs take turns doing the exercise in front of the rest of the group. The group should comment on the degree of precision achieved.

It takes a lot of practice to develop the discipline needed for total concentration—the kind that remains unbroken despite distractions. The following exercises may help.

☐ Read a newspaper article or memorize a passage from a play while your classmates talk at normal volume among themselves. How much did you accomplish? Test how well

you concentrated by reciting for the class all the lines you managed to memorize or all the details you remember from the article.

☐   Describe to the class a personal possession—a notebook, an article of clothing, a ball-point pen—in detail. The more details you find, the greater will be your involvement and concentration.

☐   Divide into two or three groups, each group forming a circle. One person calls out a single word; the next repeats the word and adds another; the third person repeats both words and adds a third. Continue the series around the group, eliminating those who cannot repeat all words in the sequence. (You can also use letters of the alphabet out of sequence, rhythmic hand claps, numbers out of sequence, vocal sounds like ''er'' and ''ugh.'') Repeat the exercise every few days until no one has to drop out. Then combine your groups and repeat the exercise again, seeing if you can extend your power of concentration even further.

☐   Concentrate on one of the following actions as you perform it in pantomime.
a.   searching your room for your physics homework which is due today
b.   preparing a banana split for a customer
c.   changing a flat tire on a snowy December day

d. planting tiny seeds or seedlings on a sunny day
e. hitching a ride from any one of a variety of vehicles on a freeway

Truth and Fiction

☐ Divide the class into two sections. One is a group of campers searching their campsite for a lost watch. The other group observes.

☐ After three or four minutes, someone in the viewing group calls time and stops the action. Then that person secretly hides an actual watch.

☐ The original group hunts for it for three or four minutes or until someone finds it.

☐ The observer group reports and discusses any differences in concentration they noticed. Which time was the "camper" group more convincing? Explain why.

OBSERVATION

The world around you contains innumerable opportunities for developing another vital tool of the actor—*observation*. When was the last

time you looked closely at the face of your brother or of a parent? Close your eyes—can you describe the room you are in? Do you remember what your best friend is wearing today? How would you describe the difference between your mother's spaghetti and that served in the school cafeteria?

Through conscious observation you can collect a storehouse of materials which will serve you well as an actor.

☐ Before the next meeting of your theater class or group, concentrate on observing a number of the following everyday details—clothing, furnishings, weather, gestures, facial expressions. You can do this in your head, though some actors make a habit of taking notes on what they see.
Observe:
a. a member of your family viewing a serious TV show ... a comedy show
b. a short order cook preparing a hamburger
c. schoolmates coming off the bus in the morning and entering the building
d. you, yourself, dressing for school ... for a dance
e. you, yourself, helping out with some kind of household work

Sense Memory

By now you may have noticed that while observation is a mental activity, requiring full concentration, it also involves all of your senses: sight, hearing, touch, taste, and smell. All that you have ever experienced or observed is stored in your brain, waiting to be recalled. Exercises in *sense memory* or *sensory recall* can make it easier to call up from your inner resources the kinds of details that will enable you to create a convincing characterization.

Suppose you are playing a character who complains of being too hot on a sultry summer afternoon. You could wipe your brow while saying your line, "Whew, it's hot!" But if that's all you did, the audience might not be convinced that the heat really bothered your character.

Try to remember the last time you were too hot on a summer day. How did you feel? Did your back feel wet under your clothes? Did your

legs stick to every chair you tried to sit in? Did you feel lazy, unable to move, let alone move quickly? Were you parched and thirsty?

You've probably answered "yes" to at least some of those questions—that means your sense memory is clicking. But in addition to remembering how you *felt* in those circumstances, remember what you *did.* If you put all the sense memory experiences you can behind the line, "Whew, it's hot!" you have a better chance of convincing your audience (regardless of the time of year) that the play is taking place in July and that the main character—you—feels the heat.

Develop an awareness of your senses. Pantomime the following activities without the use of props. Each group of exercises highlights a single sense, but try to recall and re-create a *total* experience each time, using whatever other senses are also appropriate.

☐ Sight:
a. Look for a lost book in the gymnasium.
b. Look for a misplaced book in your bedroom.
c. Look for a certain book in the library stacks.

☐ Hearing:
a. Hear a thunderclap, a long roll, another clap.
b. Listen to sounds of small night creatures.

c. Listen to the blast of hard rock at a concert.
d. Hear your mother call you to lunch . . . to take out the garbage.

☐ **Smell:**
a. Pass a bakery; smell the doughnuts frying.
b. Smell a campfire, a bonfire or a charcoal fire.
c. Walk into a chem lab and smell sulphur.
d. Smell various expensive soaps in a department store.

☐ **Taste:**
a. Eat a piece of your favorite cake.
b. Taste Chinese bird's nest soup; it's better than you thought.
c. Suck on a sourball or a slice of lemon.
d. Savor the taste of charcoal broiled steak.

☐ **Touch:**
a. Feel the hot tar of the street as you're playing stickball or hockey or jumprope or whatever.
b. Unscrew a hot light bulb.
c. Stroke a hairbrush (or the teeth of a comb) with your fingertips.
d. Put your toes or fingers into an ice cold ocean, lake, or stream.
e. Remove rubber cement or airplane glue from your fingers.

Emotion Memory

Besides the vast storehouse of sense memory you can draw on as an actor, you also have a collection of past experiences—things like the argument you had with your brother this morning or the time your dog was run over when you were six. These experiences have varying degrees of emotional content. The great Russian acting teacher and director Constantin Stanislavski was one of the first theater people to apply emotion memory to acting. The technique worked so well that it has been used, with variations, by other realistic acting schools.

Whenever you feel that you aren't fulfilling the emotional demands of a role, an exercise in emotion memory may be helpful. Let's say, for example, that a character you are playing is going to be executed in a few hours and you're not sure how to show the dread the character feels. It's totally foreign to you. But is it? You've probably never been in the situation your character's in, true—but think twice before you decide you've never felt anything similar. Have you ever, for example, had an operation and dreaded it beforehand? How do you feel before having a tooth filled? What did you *do* to express your feelings? Both those experiences, although not nearly so terrifying as anticipating having your head chopped off, involve a physical threat that can't be turned aside, plus the fear of an unknown or almost unknown pain. By recalling the emotions

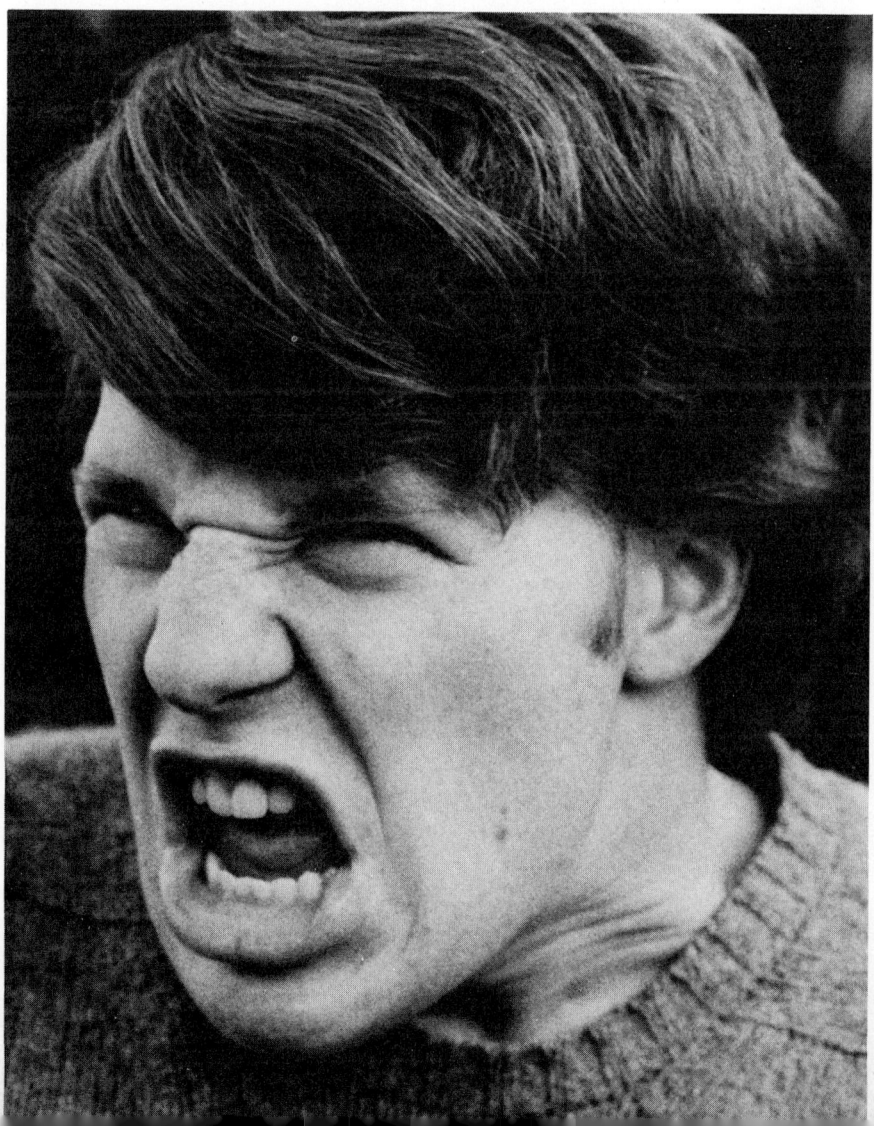

you yourself felt in a related experience, you may be able to convey what your character is going through the night before the execution.

The process of using emotion memory can be divided into steps:

1. Identify a personal experience that contains the closest thing to the emotion you want to convey.
2. Recall that experience as vividly as possible, detail by detail.
3. Allow your memory to produce the emotions you felt during the original experience and the actions by which you expressed them—crying, staring into space, laughing.
4. Transfer those recalled emotions, plus any appropriate actions, to the scene you are working on.

Although most theater people recognize the value of using emotion memory, some dislike the "substitution" aspect (step 4 above) of the technique—expecially if an actor's recalled emotion is not very close to the emotion felt by the character. For example, if an actor does try substituting the dread of having a tooth pulled for the dread of death, according to some actors and directors, his performance is not likely to be convincing.

If you're careful to substitute appropriately, however, emotion memory can be a useful tool for you as an actor. Directors too can make good use of the process during rehearsals by suggesting emotion memory exercises to actors who are having trouble portraying a desired emotion.

☐ Pair off. Pick one of the following situations. Use emotion memory to improvise the situation in front of the rest of the class.
a. A boyfriend breaking up with his girlfriend (or vice versa).
b. A parent catching a child stealing a dollar from his or her wallet.
c. A tired police officer stopping a teenager for going through a red light.
d. An employer breaking the news to an employee who is not going to be promoted after all.

☐ Each partner tell the class what memory he or she used. The class should comment on the effectiveness of the improvisation and the appropriateness of the memory each actor used. (Look for believability, appropriateness, clarity, sincerity.)

SCORING AND PERFORMING ACTIONS

The terms *actor* and *action* come from the same root. During every moment you—the *actor*—are onstage in a rehearsal or performance, your acting tools (body, voice, mind, senses, emotions, imagination) should be concentrated on an *action,* a "doing." As you prepare a role, constantly ask yourself: "What would I do *if...?*" *If I were the maid of honor or best man at a wedding, what would I do if my nose itched during the ceremony? If I were Juliet, what would I do when I first saw Romeo? If I were Romeo, what would I do when I first saw Juliet?*

A valuable device, once you've answered "What if...?" is what Stanislavski termed "making a score of the role." A *score* is simply a detailed list of every small action that makes up a larger action. Let's say you've decided that if you were Juliet seeing Romeo for the first time you would try to hide from him the fact that you liked him. A score of that action would include all the things you would do to try to conceal your feelings—avoid his eyes, smile at somebody else, fiddle with your dress.

A sample score—for the problem, "Feeding My Tropical Fish":

1. Walk into living room past aquarium, which is at center stage.
2. Stop. Look back at aquarium.
3. Look at wristwatch; see that it is 5 p.m.
4. Purse lips, raise eyebrows. It's feeding time.
5. Walk behind aquarium.
6. Stoop down a bit, tap playfully on glass to attract fish.
7. Stoop lower and locate box of fish food stored under the tank.
8. Glance at the instructions on the box for five seconds (just to make sure).
9. Open the box.
10. [You complete the list.]

☐ From the group of actions below, select one that
is familiar to you. Make a score of it and run through
it two or three times.
a. changing for gym class
b. assembling a model car, boat, plane
c. preparing something to eat (sandwich, bacon and eggs, milkshake)
d. tending or playing with a pet

☐ Now put your problem in the setting of a broader
situation. Example: problem c above:
> You've just come home from school—starved. You decide
> to prepare a snack. What's available in the kitchen?
> What will you have? Something hot . . . cold? What
> ingredients do you need? Where are they? Are there
> jars or packages to open? Are you skillful at your
> task, or clumsy? How long does it take you to make
> your snack? Do you put the ingredients away when
> you are finished? Where do you eat your snack—in
> the kitchen or somewhere else? Does it taste good?

Revise your score and begin to practice it.
(Practice—repetition—is really the only way to make perfect.)

☐ Perform your action for the class. Could they guess
what you were doing? You may want to run through
it twice, once to let them catch on to what you are
doing and once for them to analyze your performance
for logic and realism.

Moods and feelings such as anger, sorrow, hatred, pride, happiness, or whatever may be scored to provide interesting pantomime exercises for individuals or groups. Here is a group situation which calls for *changes* in mood:

☐ The football team, band, and cheerleaders are waiting
to board the bus to take them to a nearby school for

a hotly contested game. The bus ride is all fun and noise. When you arrive at your opponents' school, the teacher blows a whistle—the signal for your group to file out and line up in perfect, quiet order, ready to march onto the playing field. Each of you pick a part to play in that situation—player, cheerleader, band member, teacher.

☐ Work out and write down a detailed score for your character for each segment of the scene described.

☐ Improvise the situation, using your scores.

☐ Discuss the improvisation. Any problems? Did the scores help or hamper you when it came to working together? Can any problems you might have had be blamed on your score's being sketchy, not logical, not imagined carefully enough?

IMPROVISATION

So far we haven't talked about *voice*—but, no, you're not in training to replace Marcel Marceau, the famous French mime. Let's take a serious look at the *speaking* actor through an examination of improvisation.

We've already discussed improvisation here and there—and you've just done a couple of improvs in this chapter. Most of these, though, have been for the purpose of illustrating points about various aspects of theater or of acting. It's time now to examine improvisation for its own sake.

You can develop a whole performance from an improvisation, but for the moment think of improvisation as a training exercise aimed at developing acting skill. Through improvisation you can develop a sense of theatrical truth, logic, and believability.

Most improvisations start off with a who, a what, a when, a where, and a why; that is, a character or group of characters, a situation, time, and place, and some information about a problem that must be solved. It's up to the actors to solve the problem by using "what would I do if" to find their actions. They play (act) those actions by using sense memory, emotion memory, and all the other tools they have developed.

Make sure *before* you start any improv that you understand the situation and your character assignment. Then, during the playing, take time to *listen* and to become involved with the other characters in the scene.

In some of the exercises that follow, the *who, what, when, where,* and *why* are indicated. When they are not, the teacher, director, or actors may suggest them.

☐ Situations to spark improvisation:

a. A parent brings two children into a well-stocked pet shop, having promised to buy *one* house pet. It is a busy Saturday afternoon. Several other customers want the attention of the lone proprietor.

b. For the duration of a mass transit strike in a large city (you name it), the mayor has decreed that taxi drivers may stop to take on extra riders—"share-a-ride"—provided that all previously boarded passengers agree. It's 6:00 p.m. Each passenger has a pressing appointment.

c. The decorating committee for a Halloween masquerade dance enters a fun-and-party shop during lunch hour. They are authorized to spend $25.00. A sign in the shop reads: "Browsers Welcome! If you break it, you've bought it! When you want help, holler!"

☐ Objects for improvisation:

a. Put an object such as a knife, spoon, bell, where everyone can see it. Divide into groups of five or six persons and spend about five minutes deciding on a who, what, when, where, and why related to the object. Reassemble as a class, and each group present an improvisation based on its five *W*s. (Other objects: umbrella, wooden bowl, pressed flower, straw hat, lace handkerchief, World War II Army sergeant's arm patch.)

b. All members of the group put items from their pockets and purses onto a table. Select five or six items and use them to work up an improvisation, as described in *a,* above.

☐ Environments for improvisation:
a. A stalled elevator
b. Atop the Washington Monument
c. A computer center
d. A sea lab or bathysphere
e. An Indian burial ground

☐ Costume pieces for improvisation:
Divide into groups of four or five. Have each person bring in a costume piece from the school's costume room or from home. Using the costumes as a basis, decide on characters, a setting, and a *why*. Then do an improvisation for the class.

☐ Other improvisation starters:
a. Characters, real and fictional
b. Scenes from plays
c. Stories
d. Songs, poems, paintings
e. Proverbs, maxims, single words
f. Animals, any elements of nature
g. Colors, sounds
h. Your own mind: you name it!

By now you've probably taken part in quite a few improvs with the rest of your group. Lots of them turned out well, maybe surprisingly well. Others. . . ? But remember—in actor training, improvisation isn't an end in itself. It's only *part* of the entire process of training the actor. Since that's the case, you should follow every performed improvisation with a thorough evaluation, a critique—not so much of the whole scene, but of the acting. Answers to questions like the ones below can begin to help you judge how well you are developing your acting skills. After each improv, the audience should answer the following questions.

■ Could you follow the improvisation? Was it clear?
■ Could you hear and understand the dialogue?

- Was each actor's concentration complete?
- Did the characters seem real? Could you believe the actors' characterizations?
- Were the actors listening to one another? Were their responses as characters related to what they heard?
- Were the actors' movements and physical actions clear and logical?
- Was the improvisation inventive? Did the actors avoid cliches like, "Hi, what's new?" "How're you feelin'?" "Nice weather we're having. . . ." "How's the family?"
- Were objects (when available or allowed) used imaginatively?
- Was the dialogue meaningful?
- Did you enjoy the improvisation?

SUMMING UP

Your instrument as an actor is made up of (1) your outer resources: your voice and body, and (2) your inner resources: your mind, memory, senses, emotions, and imagination. An actor training program is much like the training program of any performing artist. It is a process of understanding and tuning the instrument through practice, practice, and more practice. You can discover a great deal about your acting abilities and you can develop those abilities by doing exercises and activities in:

Relaxation—for relieving tensions and freeing your physical instrument—your voice and body.

Concentration—for strengthening your ability to keep your mind on your character and the scene.

Observation—for making you look actively at life—into nature—for details you can apply to your characterization.

Sense Memory—for making you recall past experiences of sight, hearing, touch, taste, and smell, which help to make rich, believable performances.

Emotional Recall—for making you remember how you felt and what you *did* in past emotional experiences to help you decide what might be done by your character in similar emotional circumstances.

Scoring and Performing Actions—for making you aware of every single physical action you must do to project a three-dimensional character.

Improvisation—for involving your mind, body, and voice in a spontaneous situation where the art of listening must be added to all your other actor resources.

Activities

☐   Make up a live test you can use to check your group's progress as actors. Everyone in the group must participate in each of three ways: (1) as a designer of the test, (2) as a "taker," and (3) as an evaluator.

☐   Divide into four committees to set up the testing. Each committee select one of the topics listed below. Then read the directions on committee operation that follow.

Committee Topics

Committee #1:   Testing the solo actor. Decide on answers to the following questions.
a.   Should the test exercise be restricted to pantomime or should speaking be allowed? Should props other than chairs and tables be allowed?
b.   What types of exercises are suitable for testing an actor working alone (concentration, observation, sense memory, emotion memory, performing actions . . . other)?
c.   Should the committee provide a list of specific directions or situations for each type of exercise? (For example, if the exercise is in sense memory, some directions might be: peel a large, juicy orange and eat it; shop at a department store cosmetics counter for a just-right cologne to give as a birthday present.)

    d. Should all actors do the same type of exercise or should they be free to select one from a group of preplanned multiple choices?
    e. How long should the exercise be?
    f. Should the person tested have time to prepare the exercise beforehand, or should he or she be expected to perform impromptu—on the spur of the moment?

Committee #2: Testing actors working in a group. Decide on answers to the following questions.
    a. Should the exercise be pantomime only, or should it include spoken dialogue as well?
    b. Would improvisation be a suitable exercise for testing the actor's ability to perform with a group?
    c. How many actors should be in each improv group?
    d. Should individuals make up their own improv groups or should the groups be formed by some method of chance selection like picking numbers out of a hat?
    e. Should groups be allowed to choose their own who, what, when, where, and why? Should the test require them to select the improv idea from a preplanned group of choices? Or should they be required to pick the idea out of a hat?
    f. How long should the improvs be?
    g. Should each group tested have time to prepare the improv before the test day? Or should they be given the assignment the same day and be expected to perform after a short on-the-spot preparation period? How long should the prep period be?

      h.   Should the group be allowed to use props other than chairs and tables?

Committee #3:   Evaluating the solo actor's performance. Decide on answers to the following questions.
      a.   What method should be used to evaluate the solo actor's performance? Should this committee make comments about the individual performances in front of the entire group, or should the entire drama group participate in the critique? Should each member of the drama group be assigned one solo performer to evaluate—orally or in notes?
      b.   Should a critique follow each performance? Or should a group of performances be considered at one time? How many performances should be seen before a critique session?
      c.   What criteria should be applied in the evaluations (clarity, preciseness, originality, concentration, logic, believability, truthfulness . . . other)?
      d.   Would a duplicated evaluation form be helpful to those responsible for the evaluating? How should the form be designed (see criteria in question *c* above)?
      e.   If you use an evaluation form, should each tested actor receive copies of the filled-out form?

Committee #4:   Evaluating performances of actors working in groups. (See questions listed for Committee #3, above.)

Procedure

☐   Each committee work together for twenty or thirty minutes of class time on its assigned topic. At the end of the meeting time, select a committee member to give a preliminary report of the committee's suggestions to the full group. Invite them to react to your report: agreeing, disagreeing, making suggestions.

☐   Each committee plan a second meeting. Review your preliminary decisions. Adjust, change, and add to them as you see fit. Work toward final decisions. Write out your committee report and plan to present it to the full drama group on whatever date the group agrees to hear reports.

☐   Convene the entire drama group to hear the recommendations of all four committees. Discuss them; then make final decisions on all aspects of the test. Make appropriate assignments, set deadlines for remaining committee tasks, and choose a date for the testing to begin.

☐   During and after the testing, evaluate the performance of each actor in your group according to the standards the committees set up earlier.

☐   Discuss the test, if you like. Was it helpful? Do you feel, as actors, that you learned something useful from it? If so, what? If not, what could be done to make the test more helpful?

ACTING, LITERALLY...
How to work on a role

5

You did it! You got the part you wanted. You were so nervous when you went into tryouts that you were sure your voice was just a squeak and your knees were going to buckle at any moment. But it must not have showed, because you made it—you got the part.

Now what? Wait for rehearsal and let the director tell you what to do?

No. You can start working on your part (not memorizing your lines, however) before you go to the first rehearsal—and you'll find that you'll go on developing it in private long after rehearsals are underway.

Let's say you've already been working in class on the acting tools we talked about in the last chapter. Now that you have a part, you're going to have to apply those tools in a very special way—to convey to the audience exactly who your character is and what he or she wants in the play. For most student actors, the big question is, "Where do I start?"

The answer is—with the script. (We'll assume in this chapter that you're working with one; if you're developing your own script and part through improvisation, for example, you'll find some of the information here won't apply. But most of it will—so read on!)

The playwright has created the raw material of your character; it's up to you to dig out all the clues he or she has given you. Then you can use your own imagination to add any other information you need. You can also do research if the play is set in a specific period of history. (If you're playing a World War I doughboy or woman ambulance driver, for example, you might want to read a couple of World War I novels and look at some photographs of doughboys or ambulance drivers—that kind of research.) The important point to keep in mind is that you are responsible for creating the character the playwright wrote—that's your main job.

There are, of course, many different ways of approaching a script as an actor. You'll probably develop your own methods as you gain more experience. But for now, try these steps:

1. Read the play for the story and for the theme.
2. Read the play for ideas and specific details about your character.
3. Use your creative imagination to help your character to grow.
4. Use sources outside the script—books, photos—to enrich your understanding of the play and your part in it.

READING FOR STORY AND THEME

Your goal in the first reading will be to learn the overall plot—the *who, what, when,* and *where* of the play—and to learn the theme—the *why* of the play; its main "message." (Some actors find it easier to read the play twice, once for plot and once for theme.)

Find a quiet place where you won't be disturbed, and settle down with a copy of the script, a pencil, and some paper. Take notes as you read. These are the kinds of questions you should be able to answer:

Who are the people in this story? (A family? A group of social activists? Ancient Greek gods and mortals?)

What happens to them? (They adopt several war orphans? They save a lake threatened by industrial waste dumping? The gods teach the mortals a lesson?)

When does the action take place? (During the Vietnam War in the late sixties? During a congressional political campaign of the 1970s? In 492 B.C. during a Dionysian wine festival?)

Where does the action take place? (In the garden and living room of a simple, seven-room farmhouse in Vermont? In many locations in the town of Lakeside, Michigan? Atop Mount Olympus and in the city square of ancient Athens?)

What is the play's theme? (War is painful? political power corrupts? goodness is next to godliness?)

It is important that everyone involved in the production—in particular the actors and the director—agree on a *single theme,* a single idea of the play's core. You may find, once you get to rehearsal, that other people in the cast have ideas about the theme which are different from yours. In that case, you should discuss your views with the director until all of you agree on or at least accept one underlying idea which the production should express.

When you have finished reading the play for plot and theme, make a *script analysis*. This will (1) help you develop your understanding of theme, and (2) start you on the route to recognizing how your character fits into the play.

As you analyze the script (you may have to skim through it again), try to pay special attention to your character. For *every scene*, outline:

Where the scene takes place. (In the little rural town of Hilton, Vermont, in the Joneses' messy living room. Note the details: what state, what town; whose house, what room, the condition of the room.)

When the scene takes place. (Ten o'clock on a rainy morning in summer, 1969.)

Who is involved. (Mr. and Mrs. Jones, their daughter Elizabeth, and John Fisk, a neighbor.)

What action takes place. (John Fisk joins the Jones family for coffee. He happens to mention that his son Rob is coming home in a few days after a year and a half in the Navy.)

Notice that you have been answering, in your analysis, the same questions you answered about the play as a whole—but this time, you're answering them scene by scene, in order to be aware of what is going on every moment.

☐ Read or reread a play that has a part you'd like (or one in which you already have a part).

☐ Make notes about the play's plot and theme.

☐ Do a script analysis of each scene in which your character appears.

READING FOR IDEAS AND DETAILS ABOUT YOUR CHARACTER

In this step, you start the actual work on your character. The first thing to do is to search methodically through the script for clues to your character's personality. (Again, listing them will probably help you later on.) You can find these clues in:

- what the playwright *tells* you about your character in descriptions and stage directions
- what your character *says*
- what your character *does*
- what *other characters* in the play *say* about your character (Be sure that what they say about your character is true, however: if in a fit of anger a wife screams at her husband, "You don't have a kind bone in your body!" you can't assume that the playwright meant this to be true.
- what *other characters do* because of your character

Using only the facts recorded in the play, *make notes* of every detail about your character that you can find. Hunt for answers to such questions as:

- Who are you?
- How old are you?
- What is your height and weight?
- How is your health?
- How do you speak? Is your voice loud? Is your speech clear?
- How do you move? Are you graceful, clumsy?
- What education have you had?
- What is your cultural background?
- What is your occupation or profession?
- What is your religion? What do you believe in?
- What is your relationship to the other characters? Which ones do you like or dislike? Why?
- What is your position in the community?
- Do the other characters like you? Why or why not?
- What do you want from the other characters?
- What do you want from life?
- What methods do you use to satisfy your wants?
- What is your usual mood?
- How could your personality be described?
- How do you respond to pressure? Pain? Criticism? Praise?

It is now time for you to discover the specific scene-by-scene *objectives* of your character; what your character wants to do in each scene of the play. Look for *actions* in the script. That's not to say that your character's emotions and attitudes are not important: they must become part of your complete characterization. But emotions and attitudes are hard to act out if you think of them in general terms like *anger, sorrow, affection, contentment*. In the *Emotion Memory* section of the last chapter you were asked to recall what you *did* to express how you felt. Study the lines and stage directions for specific *actions*, for things your character *does* when he or she is expressing affection, for example: smiles gently? touches the person tenderly? looks into the person's eyes? (Later on in the rehearsal process, you will find that these outward expressions of emotion will serve you well in expressing your character's internal feelings.)

At this point, you'll find it useful to underline your lines (or your character's name at the beginning of each speech) to help you locate your lines in rehearsals and when you are memorizing.

Start with the first scene in which your character appears. Go through the script scene by scene, answering these questions to find his or her *actions* and *objectives:*

- Where was I before the scene began?
- What did I do there?
- Who was there with me?
- What made me leave?
- What do I want here?
- Is this place familiar to me?
- Whom do I meet here? Are they strangers?
- How do I behave with them?
- What do I want here?
- What do I do here?

USING YOUR IMAGINATION

So far, you have been learning about your character primarily through the information the dramatist has given you. But you can also use your creative imagination to develop a complete personality—a soul—for your character. This is where the actor's greatest contribution lies—in bringing a playwright's character to life.

It is important for you to create a character that you can believe in as well as one that is consistent with the information the playwright has given you. It might be believable for some characters to burst into tears upon hearing that a relative has died—and believable for others to try to control their grief. But for some characters, neither reaction would be obviously the "right" one. In that case, do what comes most naturally to *you*, in the role. Whenever the playwright doesn't give you exact information, it's up to you (and the director) to fill in the blanks. You can do quite a lot of this before rehearsals start, but you'll find that throughout the rehearsal period you'll continue to add details.

One of the best ways to get to know your character is to write his or her autobiography, starting with "I was born in—" and going right up till the play starts. The playwright has probably already provided you with some biographical details in the script. Create as many other particulars as you want, but be sure that they are always logical extensions of the ideas you found in the script. Provide the imaginary background for your role with such items as:

- your date and place of birth
- the names, ages, and occupations of your parents
- the names and ages of your brothers and sisters
- the names and ages of your husband or wife and your children
- the financial condition of your family
- a description of your childhood homelife
- your childhood health
- your childhood friends, pets, heroes, hobbies, favorite games, foods, tragedies, joys, etc.
- your schooling: what kind of grades you made, school activities in which you participated
- your present-day romances, friends, hobbies; favorite movies, books, foods, colors, music; things you dislike, etc.
- your achievements in life so far
- your failures and disappointments in life so far
- your sorrows and joys in life so far
- your greatest fear
- your main ambition

Try to determine what your character does when he or she isn't onstage taking part in the main action of the play. For example:

- Where do you go when you exit or the curtain falls (home, to a restaurant, to bed, to your job, to the lake, to the cellar)?
- Whom do you meet there (your spouse, your bowling buddies, a fellow conspirator, no one, the cat, your boss, a teammate)?
- What do you do there (have a picnic, quarrel with your closest friend, develop photographs, cast a spell, do the laundry, plot a murder, go shopping)?
- How much time—in terms of the play—has passed since your last appearance (ten minutes, a day, five years)?
- Why do you return to the action of the play (you've been invited, you learned that your favorite rock musician will be there, you want to stab your King to death, you want to steal a pearl necklace, you're returning home from school)?

Now, using everything you've learned and created about your character so far, see if there are any special physical or personality traits which

you can extend or enrich. For example, if your character is an elderly person, a shy person, a very aggressive person, or has any other outstanding basic trait, work on developing a posture, stance, or way of moving, and a particular way of speaking, laughing, or crying, that says—this is a shy/elderly/aggressive person standing, moving, speaking, laughing, crying. You might want to use a hand prop not mentioned by the playwright—a cane, perhaps, or a lace handkerchief—or a special costume or makeup detail. (A nervous woman, for example, might play with her jewelry; a man who's unsure of himself might be continually straightening his tie.)

If something about your character is similar to something about a person you know or have seen, you might want to model your character's mannerisms after the real-life person. Or you might want to observe people in real life in order to find details you can use for your characterization. If your character has a limp, try to study people who really limp to make sure that your limp is believable.

At this point, you may want to make a score of your character's actions for some scene that is especially important. If you haven't yet rehearsed the part and worked out your stage movements with the director and other actors, this will be only a temporary score, but it should help you to solidify some of the things you've been working on.

Some actors like to experiment with animal models. Your character might have some particular trait often associated with an animal—sly as a fox, slinky as a cat, playful as a puppy—and as an exercise in expressing these traits you might experiment with pretending you are that animal, acting out its movements, in order to find traits you can bring back to your actual characterization. Or you might think of some animal your character resembles in a more general sense—a bird, mole, cow, colt, you name it. Try running through one of your scenes as that animal. The results will be exaggerated of course, but again, you might find things you can use in expressing your character.

☐ Write an autobiography for the character you've been working on, for either an actual performance or the part you chose for the first activity in this chapter. If it's appropriate, find and develop a special way of moving or speaking for your character—but only if it's appropriate. Then read the autobiography aloud as the character might do it.

☐ Write down your character's offstage actions during the course of the play or scene.

☐ With a few other students, list a number of animal characteristics people are often given ("sly as a fox," for example). Each of you develop a character who displays such a characteristic, and work out an improvisation in which all of them meet and interact in some way.

☐ Read one of Aesop's fables and act it out with one or more other persons, changing the animal characters into human beings with the same traits.

USING SOURCES OUTSIDE THE SCRIPT

By now, your character has really begun to take shape through your study of the script and your imagination and creativity. But don't stop! There are more sources of inspiration you can use in developing your role.

Your director—listen to suggestions; try to accomplish what the director asks of you; pay close attention to all criticisms of your part and of the other actors' parts. Ask questions; tell the director what you think.

Your fellow actors—discuss the play, your role and your characterization with your cast-mates; consider their ideas; rehearse scenes, lines, and business with them outside scheduled rehearsal hours.

Other people—your family, teachers, friends, and other individuals may well provide you with ideas for characterization. A conversation with an army officer can prove helpful to an actor playing the part of Othello or any other military person; your mother or father may be an expert at expressing a parent's love for a child; your history teacher may be able to suggest information—a pictorial history book or a historical novel, for example—about the period in which the play is set.

Books, photos, and other sources—learn as much as you can about the era in which the play is set even if it's only a few years ago. You can consult books (novels, biographies, etc.), magazine articles, newspaper clippings, photographs, pictures, films, and people, in order to learn about the fashions, furnishings, sports, amusements, national events, attitudes, manners, and mores of people living in the period in which your play takes place.*

Critical comment—read everything you can find that was ever written about the play and your role. Drama critics, playwrights, directors, or actors who have played the role might well mention a small detail that will help you get your characterization.

SUMMING UP

Perhaps you are worried that all the reading, studying, researching and listing suggested in this chapter will ruin the spontaneity—the freshness—of your characterization. Nothing could be further from the truth. A complete knowledge of the play and your character will make you confident and relaxed and help you to free your body and mind to a point where you can bring your character to full life.

You—the actor—therefore, will work up your part successfully by:
reading the play to discover its plot and theme
searching through the script for information about your character's objectives, physical qualities, relationship to the theme and to the other characters
enlisting your imagination to create a complete, true, believable characterization
consulting sources outside the script to increase your sensitivity to the play and to your role

---

* See *Investigating: Gathering Information* by Jane Stine in this series for how to do period research.

Activities

☐   Divide into groups. Each group select a one-act play or a long scene from a three-act play that has rich, challenging characters.

☐   Cast the play.

☐   Read the play by yourself to find what the playwright is trying to say to the audience—what the theme is.

☐   Discuss the theme with the rest of the cast until you can agree on a single statement expressing it—and on an appropriate style for the production.

☐   Working from the script, from your imagination, and from sources beyond the script, write a thorough character study of your role.
  a. Make a list of the ways you and your character are alike physically.
  b. Make a list of all of your experiences that are similar to the experiences your character goes through in the play and in his or her ''offstage'' life.
  c. Write your character's autobiography. End it at the point where he or she first enters the play.

☐   Plan and conduct a series of rehearsals in which the cast shares responsibility for:
  a. Deciding what the setting will look like and what props are necessary.
  b. Blocking (working out) the entrances, exits, and movements of the characters.
  c. Developing the cast's characterizations and the details of playing the scenes.

☐   Present the play or scene to your drama group for their enjoyment.

☐ Participate with your group in a critique of the production. Use the following questions—and any others you can agree on as a group—for evaluating the performances and the production as a whole.

Voice and Articulation:
a. Were the voices and articulation of the actors suitable to the characters they portrayed?
b. Could they be heard and understood?
c. Did they deliver their lines naturally, appropriately?

Movement:
a. Did each actor adequately portray the age, health, occupation, personality, mood, of his or her character?
b. Were movements clear, varied, motivated? (Did they seem to spring from a definite purpose?)
c. Were the actors' bodies relaxed, but under control? Did they avoid fidgeting and other distracting mannerisms?

Characterization:
a. Did the actors maintain consistent characterizations from scene to scene?
b. Did they stay "in character" throughout the performance?
c. Were their characterizations fresh and imaginative?

Playing the Scenes:
a. Did the actors play the scenes together as an ensemble—a group? Did they listen and react satisfactorily to one another?
b. Did they achieve appropriate and consistent tempo, rhythm, and spirit in the total performance?

Overall Evaluation:
a. Did you understand the plot and the theme?
b. Were you amused, saddened, shocked, moved, bored?
c. Did you enjoy the production?

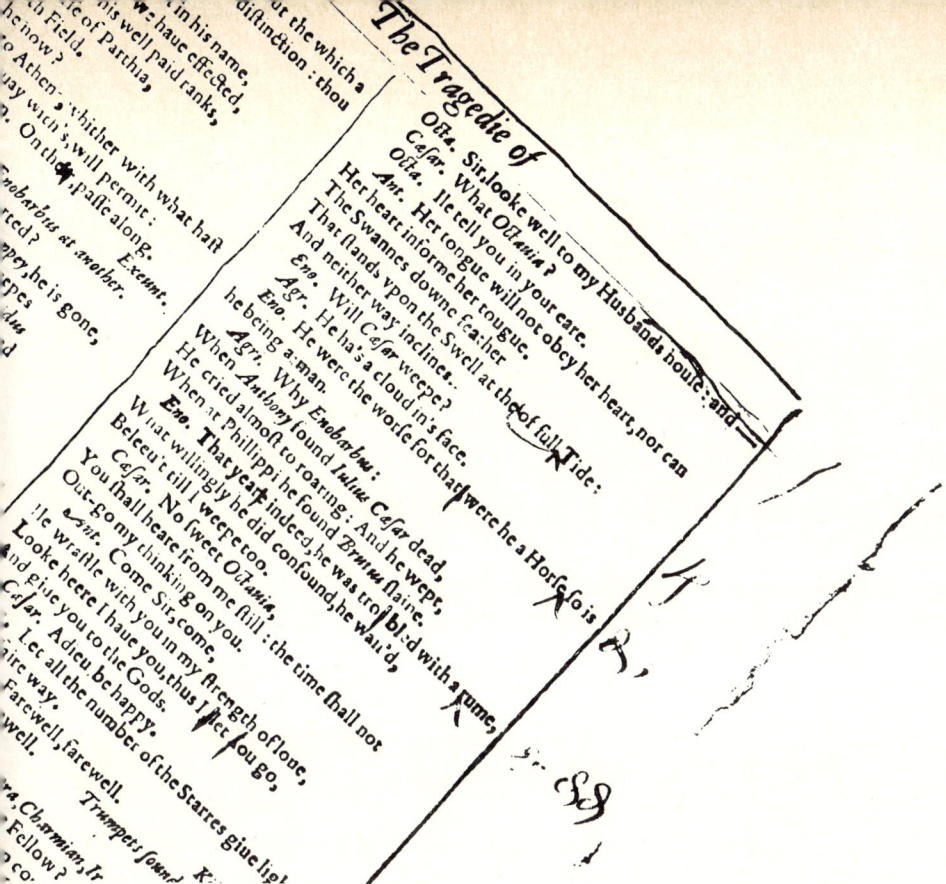

THE DIRECTOR'S ART
How to prepare to direct a play

Very few students ever get a chance to direct. That's unfortunate, because directing is the art which pulls every part of a production together—acting, scenery, lighting, costumes. Directing is an exciting, rewarding experience which anyone interested in theater should have at least once. And if theater can be anywhere—which it can—and if school productions don't have to be limited to a couple of three-act plays performed once or twice before a paying audience—which they don't—there is no reason why almost anyone who wants to can't get a chance to direct.

Almost every kind of performance needs a director, after all. You can supervise an improvisation and help actors solidify it into a skit to be performed in assembly or at lunch time. You can direct a scene two actors want to do in class. You can direct a one-act play for a dramatics club program, a children's play to take to an elementary school, a student-written play to perform in front of the English class in which it was written. Even if most major productions are directed by faculty members, there is plenty for the enterprising student director to do. All it takes is a little time, a place, a few actors, and some knowledge of how to go about it. That knowledge is what this chapter and the director's part of the following chapter will try to give you.

APPROACHES TO DIRECTING

The basic principles of directing hold true regardless of the type of performance you might be directing. In this chapter and the director's portion of the next chapter, we will concentrate on those principles, but we will also point out alternatives from time to time. Feel free to experiment with the alternatives—but make sure, before you do, that you have a general understanding of the basics. For example, if you want to hold a group discussion with the actors at the first rehearsal in order to arrive at a cooperative idea of what the play is about, fine. But you'll probably find the discussion more effective if you as director (or as chairperson) have first arrived at a clear idea of the play yourself.

DETERMINING THE PLAY'S MESSAGE

That brings us to the first and most important thing any director has to do, no matter what his or her approach is: study the script. (Or watch the improvisation if the production is to be a student-written play worked out creatively. We'll assume for now that you'll be working with a script; for more on improvisation look again at Chapters 2 and 4.)

Read the play through several times until you feel you know (1) exactly what the author was trying to communicate by writing it, and (2) what you as a director want to emphasize.

Try to grasp a mood or basic idea (or "message') running through the play. Put it in your own words and add your own ideas to it till you can sum up in a couple of sentences what you want the play to communicate to its audience. Then reread the script and see if your summary of its message fits. If not, adjust your summary until it does. Don't force the *script* to conform to your interpretation. In the theater, as Hamlet said, "The play's the thing...."

Suppose your group has picked *The Diary of Anne Frank* (adapted by Frances Goodrich and Albert Hackett) and you have been chosen director. You may feel that the play's message is "Man is unjust and cruel." Perhaps you feel that is enough of a message. But perhaps not. What makes new productions of old works (like Shakespeare's plays or the ancient Greek plays) so interesting is that each new director brings fresh insights to the script. He or she adds ideas and experiences to it, and often updates it in attitude or production style. Maybe if you are going to direct *The Diary of Anne Frank,* you might want to extend the playwrights' statement to, "Man's injustice and cruelty cannot crush a strong human spirit." But perhaps when you read the play again, you'll find that no longer works. Maybe this time around you'll decide that "The beauties of life overshadow by far man's injustice and cruelty" would be a better message. That's all right—it's better to change your mind once or twice at the beginning than to stick doggedly to an idea that might not work.

☐ Read *The Diary of Anne Frank* and see which of the themes mentioned above you think best states the message. If you were directing the play, what additional message might you be able to convey to the audience?

☐ Read a Shakespeare play (one you have already read is fine)—or any other play written a long time ago. List four or five ways in which you could update it so it would have meaning for a modern audience.

You can approach directing from the opposite angle also—you can start with a message, or with a type of drama, and find a play that fits your idea. (We talked about this in Chapter 2.) Maybe you've always wanted to communicate your feelings about drugs, or authority, or insanity to a large group of people. Then develop an improvisation around that idea or look for a play that will help you do that. Maybe you really like serious drama; perhaps you have a mental picture of a bare stage with actors moving around in stark pools of white light. Look up some of Eugene O'Neill's one-act plays, or *Spoon River Anthology* or *Brecht on Brecht*.

FINDING A PRODUCTION STYLE

When you first approach a script as a director, don't seek out only the obvious facts presented in the text. Make note of the ideas and feelings that come to you as you read. If you suddenly visualize the main character as a thin, sophisticated woman in a green dress, make a note of it. You may change your mind later, or the actress playing the part may contribute an idea you like better—but it is still important for you to get a picture of the play and characters in your mind before you start rehearsing. A professional director once said, "I never direct a play unless I can see a movie of it running through my head as I read it."

Make preliminary notes about other aspects of the production also, always keeping in mind the message you (and the author) want to convey. Will your message get across best with the assistance of scenery or can you communicate it as well—or better—from a bare stage with a few simple pieces of furniture? What about the playing area? (See Chapter 3.) What about the set? Lighting? (More on this in Chapter 8.)

Keep in mind that all the aspects of your production—scenery, lighting, costumes, the space you choose for your performance, and most of all, the actors you cast—can help to get across your interpretation to its audience. To communicate effectively, a production must be presented from a single point of view. If the lines the actors speak are funny but the scenery is dark and somber, the audience may be confused and the impact of the play lost. Having too many viewpoints is like watching TV, listening to the radio, talking on the phone, and studying all at the same time. Something—probably everything—is bound to get lost in the shuffle.

CASTING

Once you have selected your play, figured out what you want it to communicate, and jotted down some general ideas about how you're going to get it across to the audience, it will be time to select your cast. Maybe you already have a group of people to choose from—the dramatics club, your speech or drama class, or just a group of students who want to do a play. Whatever the group is, someone is going to have to decide who will play which part. You can do this yourself, with a faculty adviser, with a couple of assistants, or by a vote of the whole group. (If everyone votes, though, be careful—remind them to base their casting on talent and suitability for the part—not on popularity!)

If it doesn't matter who plays which part, you can simply ask for volunteers. You can do improvisations based on the play, and switch the parts around till the cast seems to fall into place naturally. Or you can hold *readings*—with the actors reading parts from the actual script. (See pages 10-15 in Chapter 1 for ways of conducting auditions and choosing a cast.)

One last thing you should do at auditions (or at the meeting at which you decide on parts) is give your cast some idea of how long the play will take to rehearse. This, of course, depends on how long the play is, how complicated it is, how experienced the actors are, and how much time everyone is going to be able to devote to it. As a general rule, you can allow three to four weeks of two-hour rehearsals for a simple one-act play with no sets, costumes, or complicated production requirements. For a two-act or three-act play with scenery, costumes, and all the trappings of a major production, you should allow about six to eight weeks of rehearsals of two hours each. Rehearsals should be held not less than three times a week. (See Chapter 7 for more details about rehearsal schedules.)

Before you even start your auditions, tell your prospective actors when the performance will be, how much they will have to rehearse, and what time of day you plan to hold rehearsals. Find out then and there if anyone is going to have trouble getting to rehearsals. If Susan James has to go home for lunch every day and you're going to rehearse during lunch period, you're not going to be able to use her in the play, even if she's the best actress you have. The same thing goes for people who have guitar lessons they can't miss, football practice, regular dentist appointments, or jobs.

PRE-REHEARSAL HOMEWORK

When you have cast your play, but before you start rehearsals, you still have some "homework" to do. A lot of people are going to be asking you a lot of questions at that first rehearsal. You're not going to seem like much of a director if you don't know most of the answers. Here are some of the things you should know thoroughly before you begin:

What period of history the play takes place in—today, 100 years ago, four centuries ago.

Something about the period—the clothes people wore, the kinds of houses they lived in, the kind of education they might have had. Concentrate on the kind of people your play is about—rich people, poor people, farm people, city people, and so forth. (Again, see *Investigating: Gathering Information* by Jane Stine in this series for some ideas about how to look for this kind of data.)

What the set will look like. Draw a floor plan on paper so that when rehearsals start you will be able to chalk the positions of walls, doors, windows, trees, and furniture on the rehearsal floor to show your actors the things they will have to move around or use.

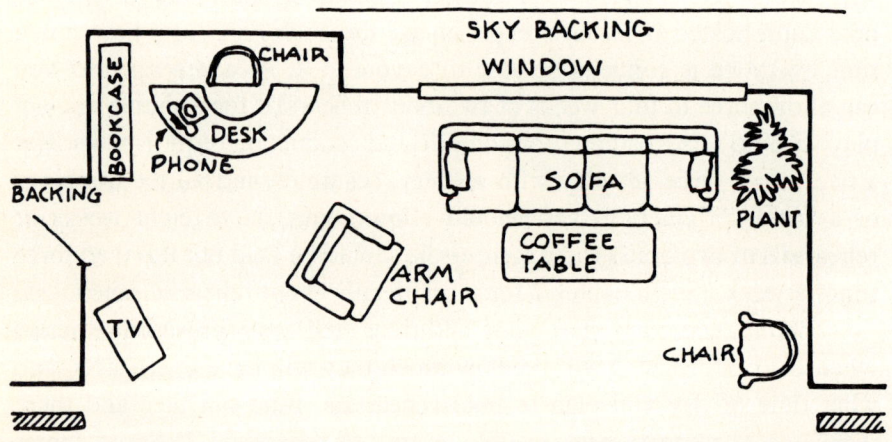

The kind of person each character in the play is. The actors will probably have good ideas about this, too, and you should certainly make use of them. But at the beginning, the actors may want you to guide them. The script will probably be your main resource here, but you may have some ideas of your own to add.

Who is going to do what on the production. Who is going to be in charge of props, lighting, costumes, etc.? Are you going to have an assistant director or a stage manager? (In many school productions, especially those directed by faculty members, the director has an assistant who attends all rehearsals, answers questions, runs errands, prompts, calls out sound effects—like doorbells or telephones ringing. He or she also serves as liaison between the director and the rest of the people involved in the production. If someone wanders into the room during a rehearsal, it is the assistant director or stage manager who finds out what he or she wants. The reason is simple: to allow the director to concentrate on directing.

BLOCKING

Another thing you should probably do before rehearsals is plan the *blocking*—the movements the actors will make onstage. (Exception: if you are working on an improvisation instead of a written script, the actors will want to work out their own movements as they go along, just the way they make up their lines as they go along. Your job will simply be to act as critic—to tell them which lines and movements are effective and which aren't.)

It is also possible to block a written script through improvisation. If you and your actors want to work that way, you can wait for the first or second rehearsal to start working out the movements. You'll work much as you would during an improvisation. The actors—scripts in hand—will read their lines aloud and move wherever they wish. You, as director, will watch and eventually tell them which movements should be "set"— used—and which should be changed. This is sometimes a very satisfying way to work: each actor feels that he or she has made the maximum contribution to the creation of the production.

The same principles apply, however, whether you are blocking the script yourself or having the actors do it. These are some points to keep in mind:

- An audience loses interest when people stand woodenly in one place on a stage and recite lines. Actors should move around the stage as much as seems natural—even more, perhaps, than they would in real life. In arena theater, make sure each actor moves periodically to each part of the stage so that the audience gets a chance to see each actor's face.
- Every time an actor moves, it should be *for a reason*. Theater people refer to that reason as the actor's *motivation*. If things get crowded on one side of the stage and you think a character should move to the other side, make up a reason for the character to move. It doesn't much matter what the motivation is, as long as it seems logical and

fits in with what is going on in the scene. A character might move to look out a window, to pick up a magazine and thumb through it, to see what time it is according to the clock on the mantelpiece. Or an actor might move to another part of the room because he or she is too nervous (the *character,* not the actor) to stand still.

- No actor should be positioned in such a way as to hide another actor from the audience.
- No actor should move in a way that hides his or her body and face from the audience. That doesn't mean an actor's back should never be turned to the audience; that can sometimes be very effective for short periods of time. But actors should not be forced by the position of other actors to turn away from the audience for long periods of time—especially if they have lines to say. Once in a while one actor will purposely "upstage" another actor. This is considered in most circles to be extremely unprofessional—and unfair, because the audience can't see what the downstage actor—the one closer to the audience—is doing.
- As a general rule, actors should move only while speaking their own lines, not while someone else is speaking.

The Working Script

As you work out your preliminary blocking, you should write it clearly in your script *in pencil* (so you can erase if you want to make changes later). It's helpful to make a *working script* at this point. (If you have a stage manager or assistant director, he or she should make one too, but that script is called a *prompt script* or *prompt book,* and should not have any blocking recorded in it until rehearsals are under way. The stage manager or assistant director will record the blocking as you give it to the actors in rehearsal, whereas you will go into rehearsals with your preliminary blocking already marked down in your working script.)

To make a working script or prompt script, either type the play on unlined notebook paper with wide margins and put the pages together in a loose-leaf binder, or, if you are using a small paperback script that doesn't have to be returned to anyone, take a copy of the script apart and mount each page on a piece of unlined notebook paper in which you have cut a "window." The "window" should be just slightly smaller than the script page; its purpose is to show the print on the back of the script page when the notebook page is turned over. The best method of attaching the script pages is to glue them firmly in place on all four sides. Don't use tape unless it's the kind you can write on easily. Use a set of index tabs to mark the act and scene divisions; start each new act or scene on a new page.

Now you're ready to start preliminary blocking.

☐ Select a short scene or one-act play and make a working script, either typed or windowed depending on whether you own the script or not. Some scene suggestions are listed below; the list of plays on page 43 of Chapter 3 offers more possibilities.

Act II, scene 1 of Terence Rattigan's *The Winslow Boy*
Act I (the first half) of Carson McCullers's *The Member of the Wedding*
Act V, scene 1 of William Shakespeare's *A Midsummer Night's Dream*

Act II, scene 2 of Christopher Sergel's *The Mouse That Roared*

Act I (the first half) of Carlo Goldoni's *The Servant of Two Masters*

One of the best ways to visualize how actors are going to look as you move them around the stage is to draw a floor plan of the set on a piece of paper, cut out shapes to represent the characters, and label them. (You can also use pennies, chessmen, checkers, or whatever else is convenient.) Then read the script, moving your "characters" around your "set" as you go along. You'll be able to see right away if one actor is standing in front of another or if everyone's crowded on one side of the stage, and you'll be able to keep track of when characters enter and exit.

☐ Make a set of cut-out "characters" and a floor plan to go with the working script you prepared in the previous activity.

As you work out each movement, record it in your script. To make this easier, you can use a "shorthand," with initials for each area of the stage. Theater people refer to the acting areas of a proscenium stage by the following terms:

Downstage—the area closest to the audience.
Upstage—the area farthest from the audience.
Stage right—the right one-third of the stage as the actor faces the audience.
Stage left—the left one-third of the stage as the actor faces the audience.
Center stage—the middle one-third of the stage.

By combining the words *up* and *down* with the words *right*, *left*, and *center*, you can form the names of the remaining acting areas: *down right, right center, up right, down center, up center, down left, left center, up left.*

Here's a diagram of a proscenium stage, divided into areas, with the shorthand initials for each section:

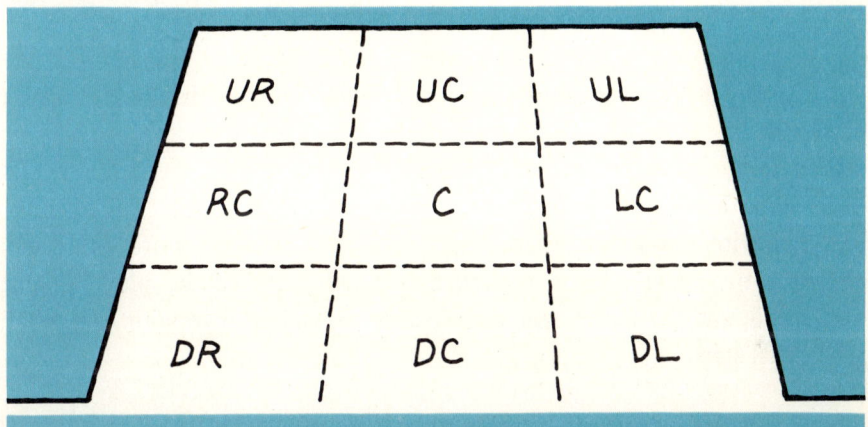

On arena stages, you can indicate stage areas by using initials for north, south, east, west, and center—or 1 o'clock, 2 o'clock, 3 o'clock, etc.

In addition to the symbols indicating place (UL, RC, NW, 9 o'clock, etc.), there's another useful shorthand symbol: "X," meaning *cross*. Take this as a symbol for "walk" or "move" and use it every time an actor goes from one part of the stage to another. XDL, then, written next to a line in a script, means that the actor speaking the line must *cross downstage left* while speaking that line.

There will be times when you will need to write more exact directions in your script than are allowed for in the simple symbols given above. You may, for example, want to say, "X 2 steps DL angrily," or, "XC, sits on sofa," or "XUL to window; opens it; calls out."

Here's a sample page of a director's script and some preliminary models to show how each movement was worked out. Notice how the movements of the small paper figures have been translated to the symbols written in the script.

MARY: (on sofa) But that's just it, John! I don't know how to tell them.

JOHN: It seems to me all you have to do is just go right up to them and--(lamely) *XL to chair —* *sit* tell them.

MARY: *X DR to window* (quietly) You see what I mean.

JOHN: Yeah. Yeah, I guess I do.

Although you can start rehearsals before you've finished blocking your play, if you're working traditionally, it's a good idea to block at least the opening scenes or act before you meet with your actors for the first time. That holds true even if your first rehearsal is simply a reading of the play with the actors sitting around in a circle. The more you block ahead of time, the clearer a picture you will have of the play in your own mind, and the better you will be able to explain it to your cast when rehearsals start.

SUMMING UP

Dare to direct a play! It's work; it's possible; it's worth it! You can direct a traditional script on your own, you can supervise an improvisation, or you can join a group in which all the participants share directing responsibilities.

Working traditionally, your directorial responsibilities might include (1) selecting the play, (2) studying it to learn its plot and theme, (3) deciding where it will be shown and in what kind of set, (4) casting the actors in roles, and (5) doing lots of homework before you meet your cast for the first rehearsal. That homework usually calls for the director to know:

the period in which the play takes place
what the set will look like
the kind of person each character is
who will help with the sets, costumes, and other technical aspects of the production
how the play will be blocked

Working improvisationally, the order of procedure will probably be (1) deciding on an idea or theme, (2) developing the plot, characters, and lines through improvisation, and (3) casting actors based on what they do during the improvs. Of course, you will need to decide where the play will be given, what the set will look like, and who's going to help out with "tech." Your responsibilities might also include deciding what theme, plot, dialogue, actions, characterizations, and technical details to "set" for the finished production.

Working democratically, your directorial responsibilities are shared with all the other actors and technicians. It's the same as being on a committee—everybody contributes ideas about all production requirements. Decisions are made by common agreement or—when necessary—by voting. The group should complete all the requirements listed in the directing approaches mentioned above—but cooperatively!

All this gets you to the first rehearsal. The director's job from the *first reading rehearsal* to the *final dress rehearsal* is covered in Chapter 7.

Activities

☐ Reread your working script, and sum up the message of the play in a few sentences.

☐ Keeping your message in mind, work out preliminary blocking, using the paper figures you have made. Record each movement in your working script as you go along.

☐ Get a group together and cast your play. Set a performance place and date. Give the actors your blocking—and, after reading the next chapter, take your play into rehearsal.

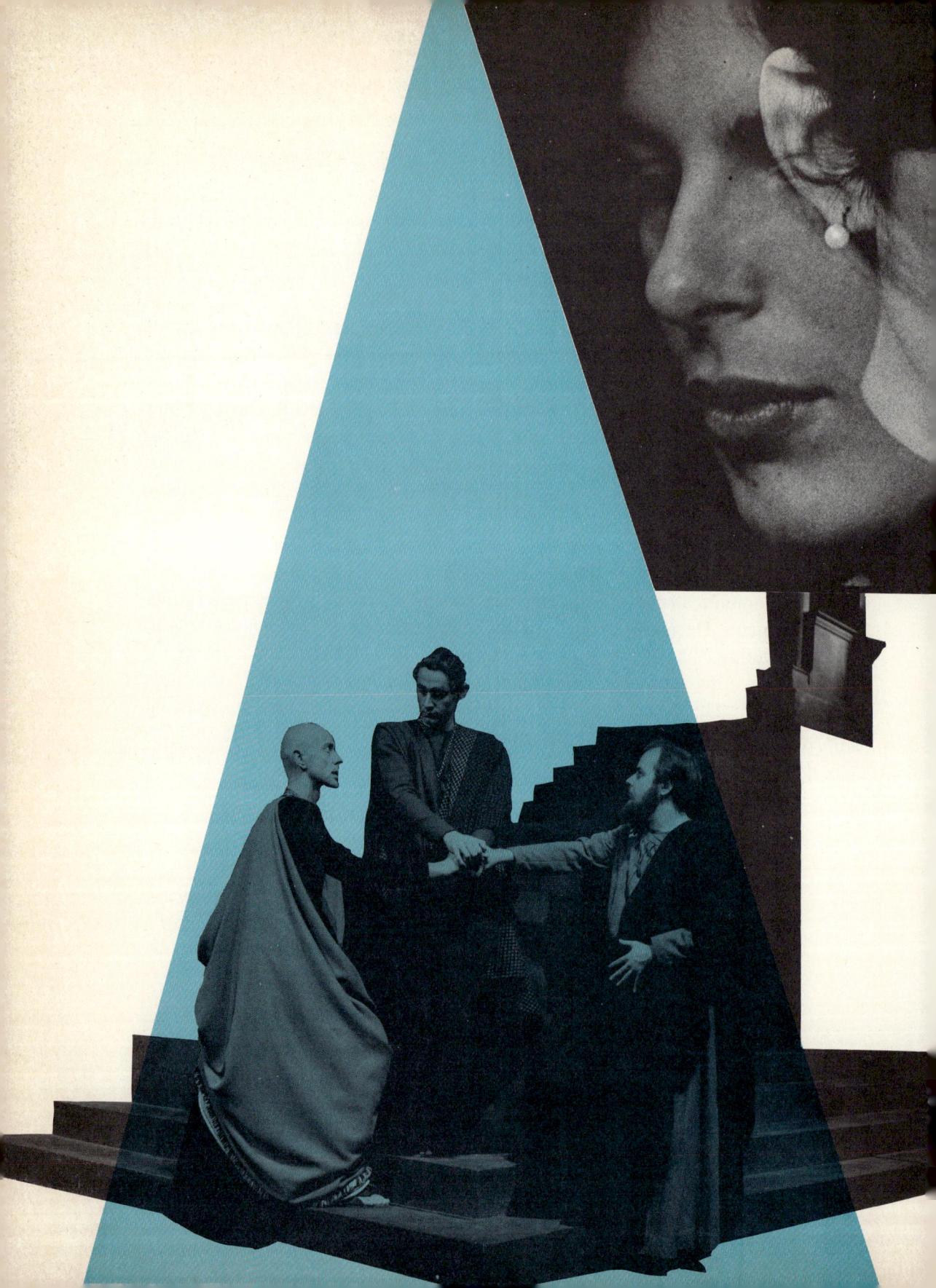

DIRECTORS AND ACTORS... IN REHEARSAL
How to work toward opening night

FOR THE DIRECTOR

A director, like the Roman god Janus, must have two faces. One sees the performance from the actors' viewpoint on the stage (from *inside* the production), and the other sees it from the audience's viewpoint (from *outside* the production).

In order to work inside the production, the director must know how to move characters around on the stage; how to make the most effective use of the physical resources of the production (sets, costumes, etc.); how to keep the action flowing smoothly from scene to scene, idea to idea and line to line; and how to help the audience to focus its attention on the ideas and actions of the play. If the director is to help with acting problems

("You say I'm supposed to be angry here, but I don't know how") he or she must know almost as much about acting as an actor: A director must understand enough about the technical side of theater, too, so there is no mystery in comments like, "I can't dim Number Five," or, "We just don't have enough braces to make that flat steady."

But a director must also deal in the intangibles of communication. A director's eye must learn to see why an action or gesture executed in a certain way will convey a certain impression. A director's ear must become attuned to the various ways the same line of dialogue can be said and the various meanings those "readings," as they are called, can convey to an audience.

This is where the second side of the director comes into play. He or she must become the eyes, ears, and emotions of the audience. Actors interpret the play from the standpoint of their characters behind the footlights. Designers and technicians see the production in terms of their own arts or crafts. Stage managers and technical crews, because of their very functions, have their attention focused behind the scenes.

The director alone sits where the audience will sit, sees and hears what they will see and hear, feels what they will feel. When the production is ready for final run-throughs, the director must come to every rehearsal as the audience will come—with no set ideas about the production, and with mind and senses ready to experience the performance "for the first time."

The director must notice and remove from the production, and the theater itself if possible, anything that will detract from the viewers' understanding or enjoyment of the play. If light leaks through a crack

in the wall of a supposedly darkened set—cover that leak! If the leading man is playing a millionaire playboy and his shoes are scuffed—get them polished! If the ingenue (a young actress in a leading role) is portraying a poor little shop girl, tell her not to wear that three-carat diamond ring her grandmother gave her. And if you suddenly realize there's so much happening onstage in a crowd scene that you can't sort out the main action, tell the crowd to keep still.

You won't be able to accomplish all these goals the moment you walk into your first rehearsal. You acquire directing skills just as you learn any skills—by getting basic knowledge and then following it with practical application. In other words, you learn to direct by directing. As you gain experience and confidence, take time out to analyze how you're doing. Find your weak points and then look for the knowledge—in books, from more experienced directors—that will help you to eliminate those weaknesses. Be brave enough to make mistakes and to change your mind. This checklist will help you evaluate your directing as rehearsals go on:

- Can everyone be seen at all times from all parts of the "house" (audience seating area)?
- Can everyone be heard and understood from the back of the house?
- Do the actors seem natural—or are their line readings and movements stiff?
- Is there some major movement for each page of the script—or are there long static periods?
- Are the positions and groupings of the actors interesting and varied?
- Is the layout of the set and its various furnishings "working"—comfortable for the cast to act in?
- Are your actors playing true-to-life, three-dimensional characters?
- Are the individual characterizations interesting and different enough from one another? Do all the characters seem to belong in the same play?
- Is your direction helping the actors to get the playwright's message across?

Any "no" answers to the above questions should let you know where you need to do more work.

Now for the nitty-gritty of rehearsing. Let's assume for the time being that you're doing a three-act play with sets and costumes—the works!

(If you're doing a simpler production, you can omit some of the material on technical and dress rehearsals.)

REHEARSALS

Try to make every rehearsal start on time. Be sure that your cast knows exactly what time they are expected to arrive, and try to hold them to it. Be sure that you and your stage manager or assistant director are there on time and ready to begin. Set a good example. If you absolutely have to be late, have your stage manager start the rehearsal by running through scenes that are already prepared. Don't lose authority and discipline by having your actors sit around waiting. They can work on their lines—there's always something constructive to do.

Plan your use of rehearsal time carefully, for your sake, for the sake of the actors, and for the sake of the production. Set a first rehearsal date and the performance dates before you begin casting if possible, or, at the very latest, when you notify your performers of their role assignments. Plan enough rehearsals to insure a good production. But use good judgment on how many. Too many rehearsals result in bored actors—that's almost as bad as having too few rehearsals. But remember the Vosburgh Law of Theatrical Production: "Any production requires forty-eight hours more of rehearsal time than is available."

When you set up your rehearsal schedule, take into consideration the demands of the play, the availability of the cast and rehearsal space, and the date set for performance. Make a full list of all rehearsals and give a copy to everyone connected with the production—actors *and* technical crew—at the first rehearsal. This is only fair; it allows them to juggle their study schedules and other activities and to notify you well in advance of any conflicts. That way, too, you may be able to adjust your rehearsal time to avoid finding people absent or unavailable just when you need them most. Your production crew will appreciate this just as much as your actors. They will especially want to know when you expect the technical aspects of the production to be ready to be combined with the acting.

At each rehearsal let your cast know what you plan to do at the next rehearsal. Will you need them for the entire time or only part of it? Are there some actors who won't have to come at all? Tell the cast exactly what will be rehearsed each time. Un-prepared actors make un-happy

REHEARSAL SCHEDULE: **The High School**

Please be prompt - 3:00 p.m.

Date:

Mon.	Read-thru of entire play
Wed.	Block 1st half of play
Thurs.	Scene rehearsal of 1st half of play
Mon.	Block 2nd half of play
Wed.	Scene reh. of 2nd half of play
Thurs.	Scene reh. of 1st half (ALL LINES LEARNED) Scene reh. of 2nd half (with scripts)
Mon.	Scene reh. of entire play (ALL LINES LEARNED)
Wed.	Scene reh. of entire play
Thurs.	Scene reh. of entire play
Fri.	Complete run-thru
Mon.	Complete run-thru (full set and all props)
Tues.	Technical reh. (full set, props, all lights)
Wed.	Dress reh. (costumes)
Thurs.	Final dress reh. (complete costumes)
Fri.	Performance - 8:00 p.m.
Sat.	Performance - 8:00 p.m.

directors. Un-used rehearsal time makes un-interested audiences. All combine to make un-fortunate performances.

An outline of traditional rehearsals follows. Most of the time you will probably do them in order—but you can always go back to an earlier type of rehearsal—a blocking rehearsal, for example—if actors need more work on something. You can, of course, combine traditional rehearsals with nontraditional ones. If your play has a long crowd scene, for example, you can schedule improvisation rehearsals with the crowd actors to enable them to develop individual characterizations and actions.

First reading — This should be an informal get-together of the cast, technical crew and director. Introduce your cast to one another, the set and lighting designers if you have them, the technical crew—everyone involved. Let them get to know one another as people and to understand one another's functions and responsibilities in the production. They are going to be spending a lot of time working together, some of it under pressure. It will help if everyone starts out being as friendly as possible.

Explain briefly your concept of the play and the production style you plan. Tell the actors what you think the play's message is and what you want it to communicate to the audience. Tell them also, briefly, your main ideas about each of the characters, stressing individual character points you wish them to keep in mind. Or, if you prefer, come prepared to hold a discussion about the play and each of its characters. Cast members should of course have read the play carefully before the first rehearsal. Each actor could prepare an autobiography of his or her character beforehand and read it aloud to the others. (It's important for an actor to have an insight into other actors' ideas about *their* characters.) Or you could all pool your ideas about each character, and let the actor decide which ideas to use and which to discard.

Show the cast (or have the designers show them) a sketch or model of the setting and any costume designs or illustrations that may have already been prepared.

Next ask the actors to sit in a circle and read through the play out loud, each person reading his or her part. Make only the stops indicated in the script—scene and act breaks—unless you feel a particular section needs explanation or discussion. Take a short break where the intermissions will be, if the play is a long one. After the entire play has been read, conduct a question-and-answer period for the cast and crew. (Or, if you prefer, and if the actors feel ready, outline the basic situation of the first part of the play, and plunge right into some preliminary improvisations based on what happens in the script. Hold a discussion after each improv to see what both you and the cast found effective. Continue working through the play this way until all of you feel ready to start memorizing lines and setting the movement.)

Before you dismiss the cast from this first meeting, be sure that you (or your stage manager or assistant director if you have one) get everyone's home address, telephone number, and homeroom number. You may need to contact someone on short notice about a change in rehearsal schedule. If the play scripts are to be returned after the production, be sure to have them numbered, and keep a list of who has which one so there can be an accurate accounting later. Rented playscripts are expensive to replace.

Blocking rehearsals — The next few rehearsals are used to work out the "traffic patterns" of the actors' movements, either traditionally or through improvisation. If you are working traditionally, first follow the preliminary blocking you've already recorded in your script, but don't be afraid to change it as you go on.

There is no need to rehearse in the actual place of performance at this point, unless it's convenient. Any area approximately the same size as the final playing area where you can work undisturbed by noise and traffic will do. Before the first blocking rehearsal, no matter what your approach, tape or chalk the floor plan of the set on the floor of the rehearsal

space (or ask the designer and/or stage manager to do it). Make this plan the same size as the real set will be, if possible. Indicate all doors, windows, steps, platforms, and any other pieces of scenery that will be in the playing space. Use chalk if you will be rehearsing in several different rooms before you reach the stage. If you will be using the same space until moving to the stage (or if you have the good luck to use the stage for all rehearsals), "draw" your plan with either half-inch masking tape or water-soluble poster paint. Either should last through all your rehearsals with only minor repairs. (Note: If you are rehearsing at school, get permission before you make any marks on the floor!)

In the rehearsal area, set up chairs and other available pieces of furniture in place of the actual pieces that will be used in the performance. Three chairs will do for a couch at this point. Don't bother with hand props yet either. (Hand props are the things handled by the actors—swords, cups, fans and the like.) The actors will have their hands full of pencils and scripts during early rehearsals. (Exception: in improvisations, with no scripts to interfere, hand props are usually a good idea.)

Explain the marked-out set and the rehearsal furniture to the cast before you begin to block. Make sure to point out all entrances and exits clearly. Have the actors make a sketch of the floor plan in their scripts for reference between rehearsals. Then begin blocking the play.

The best method, if you're working traditionally, is to start at the top (the beginning) of the first act and work through the play in sequence. This is the least confusing way; it insures that each new section will dovetail with the preceding one, leaving no loose ends.

Have the actors get up on their feet, scripts in hand, and read their lines while you call out the movements as they occur, reading from your working script and modifying your blocking whenever necessary. *Make sure the actors write every one of their movements in their scripts—in pencil!* They'll have to stop the dialogue for a minute when writing a direction—it's slow and tedious, but *necessary!* Make sure they write down each piece of "business" as well—each time they are supposed to pick up a prop or perform a small action like opening a door, drinking coffee, or yawning. You—or your stage manager or assistant director if you have one—should write each final direction carefully and accurately in the working script (or prompt book). Then, whenever a question comes up about blocking at a later rehearsal, you can be sure the answer will be available. If no one keeps track, everyone will swear to something different!

Here's how a first blocking rehearsal might start:

DIRECTOR:	When the curtain goes up, Mary is sitting on the couch. John enters from down right a couple of beats after the curtain's all the way up.
JOHN:	What do you mean, "beats"?
DIRECTOR:	Seconds, like "one, two." Ready?
JOHN AND MARY:	Yes. *(Both write their opening positions in their scripts.)*
DIRECTOR:	*(To stage manager.)* Let's go.
STAGE MANAGER:	Places! *(The cast's cue to take their positions onstage or offstage, ready to enter.)* Curtain!
JOHN:	*(Entering after a couple of beats, reading his first line from his script.)* Mary, I want to talk to you!
MARY:	*(Reading her first line.)* Oh, hi, John. I didn't see you come in.
DIRECTOR:	Okay now, Mary, on that line you get up and cross over to John. *(Mary begins to cross.)* No, not quite so far—there—that's it.
MARY:	*(Writing in script.)* Okay, I cross down right to John.
DIRECTOR:	Right. Let's take it again from John's entrance. *(John goes offstage. Mary sits on couch.)*
STAGE MANAGER:	*(Giving them time to get settled.)* Places! Curtain!
JOHN:	*(Entering, reading line.)* Mary, I want to talk to you!
MARY:	*(Rising, crossing, reading line.)* Oh, hi, John. I didn't see you come in.

And so on.

As you can see, blocking takes quite a lot of time—but it has to. It's the foundation, you might say, on which actors and director alike build the play's "body language"—the nonverbal cues that will communicate the play's message to its audience.

Block in short segments; a scene at a time, or up to a major entrance, exit, or event. Go very slowly; you're giving the actors a lot to remember. After you have blocked one section (or after everyone has agreed to blocking worked out in an improv), run through it again—a couple of times if time permits. This way the actors can get patterned into the blocking. Each time you go through, make necessary minor adjustments and refinements. Let your actors know which changes are definite and which are experiments. And unless a change is really needed, do each scene exactly the same way each time.

Never block more than one act per rehearsal. (Sometimes you may have enough time to do only half an act.) It is better to use remaining rehearsal time to rerun the act you have just blocked than to confuse the cast by giving them more than they can absorb. Save the next act for the next rehearsal. However, don't let too much time go by without repeating the previous material—certainly no more than three days—or you will find that people have forgotten your directions.

Keep working in this manner until the entire play is blocked roughly. Then you can begin polishing the movement and business in each subsequent rehearsal, concentrating on single acts and scenes if they need special attention or reworking. Otherwise, let each rehearsal be a stop-and-start run-through of one or possibly two acts. Once you've finished blocking, the actors can begin to memorize—not before. There is no one harder to direct than an actor who has memorized the script before the first rehearsal and already worked out exactly how to play the entire role.

Once the actors have started learning their lines, set a reasonable but definite date for lines to be memorized and scripts to be out of hand for each act—*not* the whole play at once—and stick to it. If memorization lags, conduct a line rehearsal or two (or ask your stage manager to). These are sit-down sessions in which the only object is the mechanical repetition of the text until everyone can recite the lines without mistakes.

Characterization and scene-playing rehearsals — One goal of the rehearsals which follow blocking rehearsals is *characterization building*. At first, the actors will play dialogue and physical action according to their

own ideas of their roles. It's up to you to approve of their interpretations —or suggest ways for them to keep the character growing in the direction you think it should. Another goal is *scene playing*. That is, the way actors perform *together*—vocally, physically, dramatically. Watch and listen to how they play their scenes with each other and make suggestions when necessary. When a scene isn't going the way you think it should, stop the actors and explain what you want. You might call out "Cut!" and follow with something like this:

"John, you must keep your 'I can't stand your attitude' speech directed straight at her. And say it quicker. Mary, come right in with your answer, but give it more sarcasm. The whole scene needs to move faster and needs more irritation from both of you to build it to a climax and show the audience how serious the conflict is between the two characters. Go back to where Mary says, 'What's so private about that letter?' and try it again."

Sometimes you will have to work with your actors on *line readings*, too—the way they say their characters' words. The most important goal here is to have everyone sound as natural as possible (unless you are purposely trying for another effect)—not as if they were reciting a memorized poem in English class. Work in private if need be with any actor who is having trouble sounding natural, and try to get him or her to vary the pitch and emphasis of a given line. If, for example, an actor is saying

-GOOD-MORNING-BILL-HOW-ARE-YOU-

giving each word equal emphasis and saying all the words on one pitch, make a drawing of how you want the line said:

```
GOOD                                            you?
        ning, Bill. /pause/   How're
   mor-
```

If that doesn't work, say a *similar* line yourself, and ask the actor to imitate you. Then have him or her try giving the same inflection and emphasis to the line in the script. (As a last resort, but only much later on—during the final week of rehearsals, let's say—if the actor still isn't giving you the line reading you want, then say the actual line from the script yourself and have the actor imitate you.)

Improvisation often helps loosen actors up. If the actors feel a scene doesn't quite make sense, or if a bit of blocking seems awkward, or if they feel uncomfortable at some point in the play, have them do an improvisation of the trouble spot, keeping the characters and situation the same, but improvising their lines and movements. Then try running the real scene again, changing the blocking if necessary but keeping the real lines intact. Chances are the actors will return to their old lines with more understanding and will be able to read them more successfully.

As soon as the scripts are out of hand, the actors will be ready to work with rehearsal props or substitute props. (The real ones probably won't be available yet.) Be sure that you have something at rehearsal to represent all items that are handled by each actor, so that he or she can become accustomed to working with them. At this time, too, have your performers wear rehearsal clothes that approximate their actual costumes. If your leading lady will be wearing hoopskirts, don't let her rehearse in jeans and sneakers at this stage. Have the actors get used to such unfamiliar pieces of costuming as swords, trains, heels, long robes, and so on. After all, only the audience should be in for surprises during the performance, not the actors! Remind the actors that onstage, clothes can help make a character come alive. People move and feel differently in various styles of dress. Use this to good advantage during your rehearsals.

Act and play run-through rehearsals — By now, the blocking, characterizations, and interpretation of the scenes should be coming together. You are ready for a series of nonstop rehearsals—run-throughs. Plan a couple of run-throughs for each act to get it to run smoothly and to get the staging pretty much set. Then schedule several complete run-throughs in which you do the entire play straight through without interruptions, using rehearsal props, furniture, and rehearsal costumes. Take breaks where the intermissions will be to accustom the performers to the flow of the play. This will help them learn to pace themselves through the performance.

While you watch a run-through, try to do it from the point of view of an audience member, using that "outside" part of a director that we talked about earlier. Take notes about anything that needs more work. Then, when rehearsal is over, assemble your cast and go over your notes out loud in the presence of all the actors (except for any notes which are of an extremely personal nature). A note to one performer may affect several others. For example, if you say: "John, that slap you give Mary was not very convincing. The next time I really want you to belt her one!" it might be a good idea for Mary to be ready for it. (Your stage manager or assistant director should hear your notes also, for he or she will be responsible for making sure your direction is followed during performances.)

Here is what one page of a director's notes might look like after a first run-through:

> Act I, Scene 1
>
> John — late entrance (<u>couple</u> of beats, not <u>ten</u>)
>
> Mary — don't rush 1st line — MORE SARCASM
>
> John — put pistol on DS end of desk. Don't sit until "I won't <u>stand</u> for it"
>
> Susan (stage manager) — get better pistol from props by next TUES. — want higher desk chair
>
> <u>Mary's reaction to gun good</u>
>
> Butler — LOUDER!! — exit faster — be out of room by "Very good sir"
>
> John: <u>really slap her</u> ~ say "wash" not "<u>warsh</u>"
>
> J & M — apology scene <u>worked</u> — bravo! ★

If you are working with an improvisation instead of with a written script, you will probably conduct most of your rehearsals like run-throughs. You might sit "out front" from the earliest rehearsals on, taking notes while the actors go through the lines and movements they have made up. After each run-through of the improv, you can give the actors your notes, telling them what you think needs changing and what should stay as is. You might want to do partial run-throughs of places that need work—but for the most part, if your production is to be truly created by

111

improvisation, story and all, the director should intervene as little as possible. Lines and movements in an improv—even a "set" one—can vary slightly from rehearsal to rehearsal and performance to performance; the message and general plot structure are usually the only things that remain entirely the same.

By this time in a traditional production, the sets, lights, costumes, and props should be ready to work with. It's at this point that you can transfer your rehearsals to the actual playing area or stage and begin technical rehearsals.

Technical rehearsals — The purpose of a "tech" rehearsal is to coordinate the performers and your direction with the technical aspects of the production. Every light cue, every sound effect, every costume and set change, must be rehearsed so that it fits in smoothly with the action of the play. Techs are long and tedious for all concerned, but they're necessary if everything is to go smoothly during performance. Don't be surprised if you don't get through the entire play in one rehearsal. The more complex the production, the more time will be required. Start at the beginning and work from cue to cue, solving problems as they arise, or at least make note of what the problems are so that they can be solved before the next rehearsal.

If you have a stage manager, it is at the first tech that he or she should move backstage and take command of the crew. In rehearsals, the stage manager was probably the one who said "curtain" and improvised sound effects when they were due—but now it's the stage manager's job to actually pull the curtain (or see that someone else does it) and to make sure the sound person plays tapes, rings bells, and shakes thunder sheets on time.

Let your stage manager and/or crew members (or designers and technical director, if you have any) be your advisers during this phase. They are working with the actual equipment while you are sitting out front in a comfortable chair. The tech staff will know best what the problems are and may have the best answers as to how to handle them.

Don't expect polished performances from your actors during techs. They're going to be coping with a lot of mechanical things for the first time, and these will demand their attention until they get used to them and can integrate them with their acting. They'll get it all together again as soon as they're at home in their new environment.

Remember, while you're doing technical rehearsals, that you'll still have the dress rehearsals in which to work with the cast. Many tech problems can be worked out by the stage manager and crew without the presence of the actors. You may even be able to turn a tech rehearsal or two over to your stage manager and give yourself and your actors a well-deserved afternoon off.

Dress rehearsals — Dress rehearsals are performances without the audience. Treat them as performances. Let your stage manager or assistant director run the show backstage. Give the actors a forty-five-minute "call" before the rehearsal—require them to be backstage at least forty-five minutes before curtain time so they can get into costume and makeup and find out where backstage their hand props will be set—placed ready for them to pick up. Make sure that the actors move and speak *exactly* as you have directed. The point of a rehearsal is to rehearse what you are going to do during performance, not what you aren't going to do!

Don't insist that the cast wear makeup at every dress rehearsal (if you have more than one), but ask them to use it at least once so any necessary corrections can be made before the actual performance.

If there is no one in your group who knows how to use stage makeup, make sure there is someone around before dress rehearsal who does, and

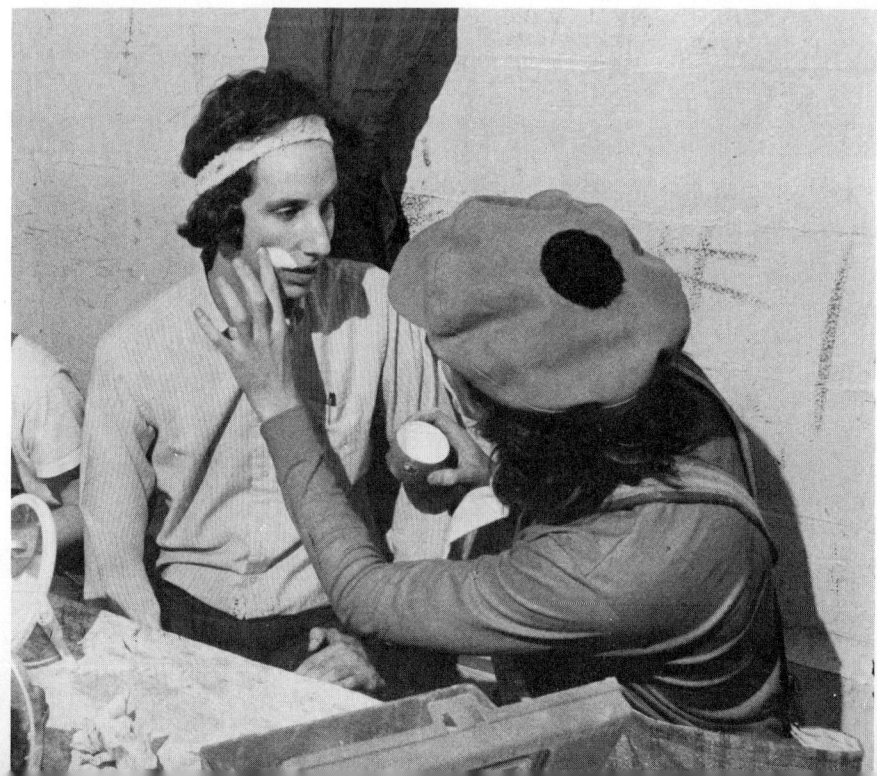

have that person make the actors up. Remember that there are a lot of differences between stage makeup and street makeup—and remember, too, that complicated makeup (old age, monsters) takes a long time to put on.

Don't schedule too many dress rehearsals, even if you have the opportunity, or you will risk destroying the spontaneity essential for a fine performance. Three dress rehearsals are plenty. The last one (the "final dress") might have a small invited audience to give the actors a taste of audience reaction. This is an especially important consideration in comedies, when the actors will have to get used to waiting for laughs.

Follow each dress rehearsal with a "notes" session. *Everyone* involved with acting in or running the production (stage manager, crews—or at least crew heads) should be present. Go through your notes an act at a time, and when you're finished with each act, invite the stage manager and crew heads to give any notes they wish, especially when the notes have something to do with the actors' relationships to the technical aspects of the production.

The master carpenter (person in charge of shifting the set) might say: "Between scenes one and two of the first act, it would be better for the actors to clear off to stage right, because we're bringing in two pillars from stage left and the traffic jam gives us a time problem."

The property master might say: "When John bangs that gun on the desk, could he hit the blotter instead of the wood? It's a borrowed desk"; or, "When actors walk off the stage with props, they *must* put them on the prop tables in the wings—not in the dressing rooms—if they want to find them tomorrow."

The wardrobe mistress might say: "If Mary will give me her skirt, we'll shorten it a bit so that she can move around more freely."

The stage manager might say: "Actors, please stay out of the wings and off the stage until places are called. The crews need all the room they can get for making the shifts. Also, tomorrow's call is for seven o'clock."

And so on. It's not only polite to give the stage manager and crew heads time to talk to the company—it insures the well-coordinated, smooth-running production you want!

Curtain calls — Believe it or not, curtain calls have to be blocked and rehearsed just like any other onstage action. There's nothing worse after a terrific performance than for the curtain to open while the audience is clapping enthusiastically—only to reveal one or two embarrassed actors frantically beckoning to their fellow cast members to come on stage.

An easy way to stage curtain calls is to bring your cast on one at a time, each one entering from alternate sides of the stage. Let the least important character enter first—say from up left—cross to down center, bow, continue crossing to the opposite side of the stage (down right) and wait just behind the curtain line. As soon as the first actor has bowed, the second should enter (from up right this time), cross to down center, bow, and continue his or her cross to the opposite side of the stage. Continue bringing your actors on one by one until everyone is on the stage. Then the whole cast should bow together (that's called a "company bow") and the curtain should fall. *Period*—unless there's tumultuous applause, in which case the stage manager should bring the curtain up again quickly for another company bow.

The key to good curtain calls—and to keeping the audience enthusiastically clapping—is to keep your calls simple and fast. Assign the actor who ends up in center stage to lead company bows; whenever everyone bows together, they should take their cue from that performer. That way, there's a better than average chance that everyone will bow at the same time.

Make sure everyone in the cast knows the sequence for the calls as well as they know the rest of the show. Rehearse them at your dress rehearsals until no one makes a mistake. And make sure everyone knows that the number of curtain calls is up to the stage manager (or whoever is pulling the curtain if there is no stage manager). That person and that person alone must gauge the applause and signal the cast when to stop the bows. Otherwise—chaos!

FOR THE ACTOR

The biggest responsibility an actor has is to his or her role. The director can tell the actor when and how to move, other actors can (and often do) make suggestions about line readings—but in the final analysis, each actor alone is responsible for his or her own performance. Because of this, what an actor does between rehearsals can be as important as what he or she does during them. Most of the work on characterization, most of the thinking, the experimenting with line readings, the trying-to-get-inside-the-character's-skin—as well as most of the memorizing—has to be done outside of rehearsals. Rehearsals are for *testing* the things that seemed successful while you worked on your role at home. They are for relating to the other actors who will be onstage with you and for meshing your performance with theirs. They are for *listening* to the other actors' lines, for *concentrating* on the action of the play as it unfolds—and for getting the most out of what the director says to you, even if some of it is negative.

Criticism can be hard to take, but it is the only way a director can tell you what is working and what is not. If a director tells you that you shouldn't cross on a certain line, or that you should sound angrier when you say, "Get out of here, Sturdley!" try not to take it personally. The director is watching your performance from the same perspective as the audience will be watching it from later, and is trying to help you get across to them. No actor can watch himself or herself adequately. Try to remember that the director's on your side and that only the director can pull all the individual pieces of the production together into a meaningful whole.

The most important thing for an actor to do at rehearsals is to pay attention to what's going on and to at least try to do everything the director suggests. If you can't do it, or if it doesn't work, chances are the director will be the first to want to make a change. If not, and you're asked to do something you disagree with or feel uncomfortable doing, talk to the director about it after rehearsal. In the meantime, try to think of an alternative to suggest.

The tough internal work an actor does outside rehearsal has been covered in Chapter 5. Here, in list form, is a summary of an actor's main rehearsal responsibilities.

TO PREPARE FOR THE FIRST REHEARSAL:
1. Read the script, but don't memorize your lines. Try to get a clear picture of the play in your mind and a general idea of how your character fits in.
2. Underline your lines—or your character's name each time it appears. That, as we said before, will make it easier for you to find your lines while you're still reading from the script, and will help alert you to entrances.
3. Know when and where all rehearsals are to be held. It's your responsibility to find out. Keep a copy of the rehearsal schedule in your script or a notebook. Know what is to be rehearsed and what is expected of you—and be ready to do it. If you must be absent or late, tell the director (and the stage manager or assistant director) well in advance.

AT READING REHEARSALS:
1. Take notes on anything that pertains to your role, the play in general, and your rehearsal responsibilities.
2. If the director has the cast read through the play aloud, read your part loudly and clearly. Concentrate not so much on characterization at this point as on reading your lines for their meaning.
3. If improvisation is used to explore the play, or to create an original one, contribute everything you can to characterizations and to the theme and structure.

AT BLOCKING REHEARSALS:
1. Bring several sharpened pencils with erasers—*no pens*—a notebook, and your script. (Bring these three items to *all* rehearsals—even after you have memorized your lines—and bring them to performances too.)
2. Copy into your notebook, a sketch of the director's floor plan for each scene and act when it is shown to you. Keep the sketches in your script or notebook.
3. If the play is being blocked traditionally, *write all your movements and business* in the margin of your script nearest to the line where the action is to be done. (See Chapter 6 for "shorthand" symbols that will make

this easier.) Stick to the blocking you are given unless the director agrees with a change you suggest.

4. Speak your lines clearly and execute the movements as efficiently as possible.

5. In your notebook, begin to keep a list of the props you will use in the play. Add to the list as necessary.

AT CHARACTERIZATION AND SCENE-PLAYING REHEARSALS:

1. Apply all the decisions you've made through your earlier character analysis to each of your scenes.

2. Throw yourself completely into your part and play each scene as effectively as you can.

3. Listen attentively to what the director wants from you. Try to make it part of your interpretation of your role. Of course, you can't act out effectively anything you don't understand, so when necessary, ask questions. (You should feel free to ask questions at any rehearsals, for that matter.)

4. If the director has asked you to "have your lines down" (that is, memorized) by this time, then have them down! When you forget a line, just stop in place, keep in character as best you can, and call out, "Line!" The person holding the prompt book will read the line—or part of it—to you. Then continue the scene. (If you're still shaky on lines, study them; when you're not needed on stage, ask another actor or crew member to go over them with you.) Pick a place to work in where you won't disturb the rehearsal.

5. You will be using rehearsal or substitute props by this time. Handle them for practice and while you are actively rehearsing, but return them or leave them wherever you're supposed to.

6. If rehearsal costumes are required, have them on in time for your scenes.

AT RUN-THROUGH REHEARSALS:

1. *Have your lines down cold!*

2. Play your scenes with complete concentration. Bring to your characterization and to the play all that you've learned from your own study of your role and from your director.

3. Stick to the lines, blocking, and interpretations that have been agreed

upon so far. Any "playing around" with these things can throw a fellow performer off.

4. Keep your scenes moving. Pick up your cues (that is, don't let there be dull pauses between the last actor's line and yours).

5. Listen carefully to all the notes the director gives to the other actors as well as to those intended for you personally. Naturally, your questions and ideas are always welcome—but don't be picky and temperamental in these discussions. Accept the fact that the director sees the whole picture of the production. He or she is the final judge. Trust your director.

AT TECHNICAL REHEARSALS:
1. Familiarize yourself with the set and with your props before the actual rehearsal begins. But don't interfere with the crews; they are probably busy getting ready for the tech run-through. If something you must use is complicated or fragile, have the appropriate crew member teach you how to handle it.

2. Learn where your personal hand props will be set and where you should return them.

3. Find out where backstage you will be safe and out of the way of the crew during scene shifts. Learn where that place is and "memorize" the location as part of your backstage blocking. It's best not to be a backstage wanderer.

4. Respect the backstage crews. During techs (and dress rehearsals and performances too), take your problems to the stage manager or whoever is in charge backstage, and follow his or her instructions.

5. When notes are given after the tech, listen, ask your questions, and record in your notebook whatever pertains to you.

AT DRESS REHEARSALS:
1. Be in the theater in time for the call. Write your name on the attendance sheet if there is one, and then go to the area assigned to you for getting into your costume and makeup.

2. Check to see if *your* offstage props are in place. Resist the temptation to fiddle with them or with props assigned to other actors. By no means should you walk off with any prop. Ever try to shoot someone with a missing gun?

3. Play your part as though your best friend, your favorite teacher, your parents, and a Broadway talent scout were in the audience.

4. Really, really *LISTEN* to the after-rehearsal notes given by the director and the tech staff. By now, hopefully, you have all the answers and no questions. (B-u-u-ut, if you *must* ask. . . .)

5. Go home and get a good night's sleep, so that you'll be rested and fresh for opening night!

SUMMING UP

It is the director's job to organize and conduct a series of preplanned rehearsals designed to guide and coordinate the cast in a way that will assure the best possible production. He or she may work traditionally—

from a set script, reserving all the decisions to him- or herself. Or the director may work improvisationally, allowing a great deal of cooperative "direction" to come from the entire cast. Whatever approach is used, the director and the actors, with or without the aid of a stage manager or assistant director, will go through a rehearsal period designed to accomplish:

> an understanding of the play and the characters
> a logical pattern of movements and actions
> creative interpretations and characterizations
> a sense of playing scenes together
> smoothly executed run-throughs of whole acts and the whole play
> a successful interweaving of the technical aspects of the production with the spoken play
> a happy and cooperative spirit, an integration of all the actors and technicians in the company

Activities

You may have noticed there were no activities in this chapter. That's because by now your group should be ready to do a play. So:

☐ Pick a play and a date for performance. Pick a director. Pick the actors. Pick designers. Pick a stage manager, or an assistant director. Pick the crew heads. Pick the crews.

☐ According to your title or role, plan what you are responsible for.

☐ According to your title or role, execute and accomplish what you are responsible for.

☐ Perform the play!

☐ How did you do?

THEATER TECHNOLOGY
How *not* to be confused by production

"When the blues on the cyc dim out, freeze until the house curtain falls. Cross up right to the ground row, pick up your hand props, then cross to the down left trap."

Sound like a different language? The words are English, but they're the jargon of the stage. Whether you are an actor or a director, you will want to know enough about technical theater so you won't feel lost. The purpose of this chapter is not to teach you how to be a technician or how to achieve technical effects, but to help you become familiar with the major technical elements of theater—scenery, props, lights—and, very important, to introduce you to the stage crew and their vital jobs.

123

THEATERS

The Proscenium Stage

Your school, as we said earlier, probably has a conventional auditorium—one where the audience sits in a basically rectangular section and views performances given from a raised stage set into the wall at one end of the room. A theater that is arranged in this way is called a proscenium theater and its stage is referred to as a proscenium stage (see Chapter 3).

There are two major sections in a proscenium theater: the *house* (auditorium) and the *stage house*.

The *house* includes some or all of these areas:

- The *orchestra pit*—the area just below the stage, sometimes sunk below floor level. It is, as you can guess by the name, where the orchestra sits in musical productions.
- The *orchestra*—the main seating area.
- The *balcony*—also referred to as the *loge;* a seating area on the upper level of the house. Of course, some theaters do not have a balcony and some have more than one.
- The *projection booth* or *light booth*—a small room, usually at balcony level, at the rear of the house from which films can be shown. It may also be used for operating spotlights and special effects projectors, and for housing the lighting control system—the switchboard.

The *stage house* includes the stage and all its parts:

- The *proscenium arch.*
- The *apron* or *forestage*—an extension of the stage floor, extending a few feet into the house beyond the proscenium arch.
- The *fire curtain,* sometimes called the "asbestos curtain"—a curtain, often required by law, hung directly behind the proscenium. It can be dropped to separate the auditorium from the stage house in case of a smoke or fire emergency on stage.
- The *house curtain* or *act curtain* or *grand drape*—the main curtain, often made of a heavy velvet or velour fabric. When it parts in the middle and each half is drawn to opposite sides of the stage it's called a *draw curtain* or *traveler.* When it can be raised or lowered straight up and down behind the proscenium arch it's called a *drop curtain* or a *jacknife curtain.*
- The *teaser* or *grand valance*—a short strip of curtain hung behind the top of the proscenium. It can be lowered a little to reduce proscenium height. It is generally made of the same material as the house curtain and is usually hung just in front of it to help hide overhead lighting equipment when the house curtain is open.
- The *tormentors* or *torms*—curtains or cloth-covered wooden frames behind the sides of the proscenium. They help hide the backstage area.
- The *traps*—some stage floors are equipped with trapdoors through which actors or scenery can be moved for special effects.
- The *wings*—all offstage and backstage space which is out of view of the audience during a performance.

☐ The following diagrams represent a typical proscenium theater. Study the various parts of the drawings. Take a tour of your school auditorium and identify as many items as you can.

☐ Tour another theater, a concert hall, an old movie theater. Again, identify as many items as you can.

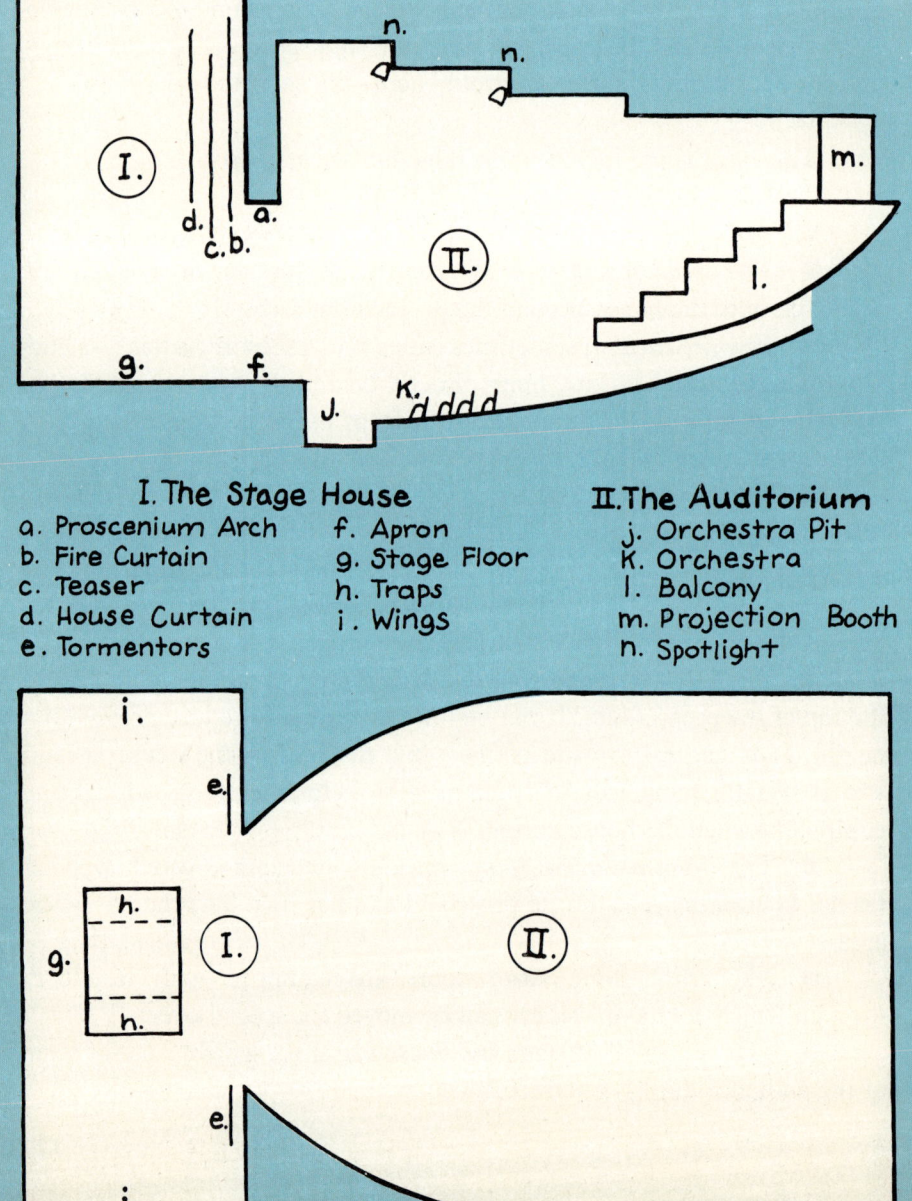

I. The Stage House
a. Proscenium Arch
b. Fire Curtain
c. Teaser
d. House Curtain
e. Tormentors
f. Apron
g. Stage Floor
h. Traps
i. Wings

II. The Auditorium
j. Orchestra Pit
k. Orchestra
l. Balcony
m. Projection Booth
n. Spotlight

The Thrust Stage

If you had gone to see a Shakespeare play in Elizabethan days, you might have watched the performance from one side of the stage instead of from the front. Have you ever been in a modern theater where the stage apron extends out into the house? A stage of this type, modeled on those used in Shakespeare's day, is called a thrust stage. They are becoming increasingly popular today because they make it possible for the audience to be brought close to the action of the play. Two professional theaters which are equipped with thrust stages are the Tyrone Guthrie Theater in Minneapolis, Minnesota, and the Vivian Beaumont Theater, which is part of Lincoln Center in New York City.

The Arena Stage

Theaters like the Arena Stage in Washington, D.C., and New York City's Circle-in-the-Square are designed with their stages in the center of the house, surrounded on all sides by audience seats. Theater using an arena stage is called arena theater or theater-in-the-round.

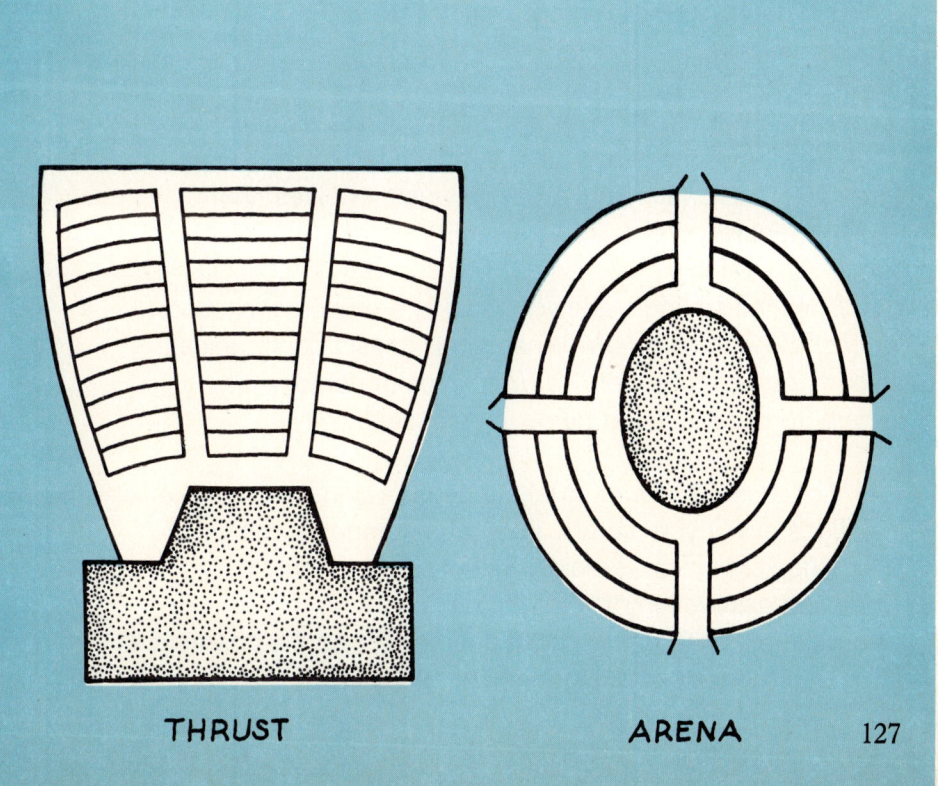

THRUST　　　　　　　　ARENA

SCENERY

Sometimes a playwright will ask that his or her play be presented on a bare stage—without scenery. Sometimes, too, a director or designer will decide that a bare stage will communicate just the right feeling of starkness or simplicity for a particular production. For most productions you work in, however, you will probably have some type of scenic background. Bare stage, partial set, or complete set—the purpose of each is to help to get the playwright's message across to the audience. Scenery can help you, as an actor or director, communicate to your audience about:

- the *locale*, the place in which the scene is set
- the *time* or period in which the action takes place
- the *characters* or a principal character of the play (The set for the living room in Moliere's *The Miser*, for example, might be simple and sparse to accentuate the stinginess of the main character—a miser.)
- the predominant *mood* of the play (If your play is a comedy, the set will probably be decorative and painted with cheerful colors. For a tragedy, your set is apt to be heavier, more oppressive, and painted with darker colors.)

☐ Search through magazines for color pictures of "settings"—not real stage sets, but places such as rooms, streets, forests, waterfront areas, villages, or cities, that a playwright might choose as a setting.

☐ Does the setting make you think of a particular situation or of some kind of action? What mood does it communicate (gloom, cheerfulness, etc.)? What kinds of personalities (characters) might be at home in each setting?

☐ Visit an art museum or take a book of prints of paintings out of your library. Look at a number of paintings which depict places or rooms. Select one and write a one-page description of what the painting says to you about time, place, action, dominant mood, and the characters who are shown or who might inhabit the scene.

There are many types of scenery. Depending on the demands of the play, the kind of stage it will be performed on, the ideas of the director and set designer and—in many cases—the money available, your scenic background may be complete and elaborate or fragmentary and simple. It may be realistic or it may merely hint at the locale or atmosphere. A living room set, for example, could include real-looking walls with pictures hung on them, furniture, windows and doors, vases of flowers and the like—or the living room could be suggested by means of a table, a vase containing a single flower, and a couple of chairs, all placed on an otherwise bare stage.

Standard Scenery Units

You've probably already seen a number of standard scenery units such as flats, draperies, backdrops, and the like on your school stage. These descriptions will help you to review what each one is:

The *flat* is perhaps the most basic unit of scenery. It is a rectangular wooden frame, one to six feet wide and ten to eighteen feet high, over which a fabric (usually canvas or muslin) is tightly stretched, fastened down, and painted. A narrow flat—one under about thirty inches wide—is called a *jog*. The surface of a *plain flat* has no openings in the fabric; plain flats are usually fastened together to represent walls. Special purpose flats, such as the *door flat*, the *window flat*, and the *fireplace flat*, are combined with plain flats to make realistic settings. Because flats are solid, they are not used in arena theater.

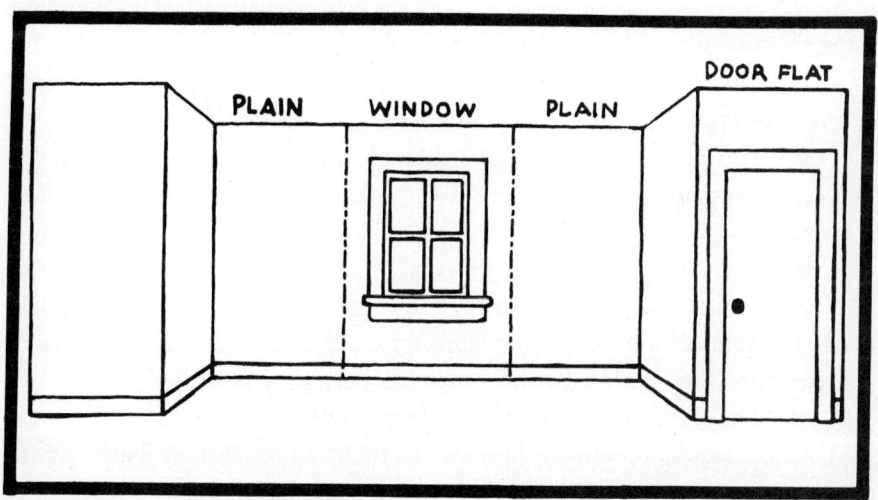

Stage draperies, usually called *drapes,* are heavy fabric hangings which are standard equipment on most proscenium stages, especially in schools. They serve to hide the backstage areas from the audience and generally "dress up" the stage. Drapes are usually attached by tie lines (cords) to pipes or strips of wood (battens) which hang above the stage.

A complete set of stage draperies would include the following items:

■ A *panel*—the widest section; used to mask (hide) the back wall of the stage.

■ *Legs* (at least two)—narrow sections; used to mask the wings of the stage, as tormentors do. On some stages, the tormentors actually are drapery legs.

■ A *border*—a wide but short section of drapery—like a teaser—used to mask the equipment hung over the acting area.

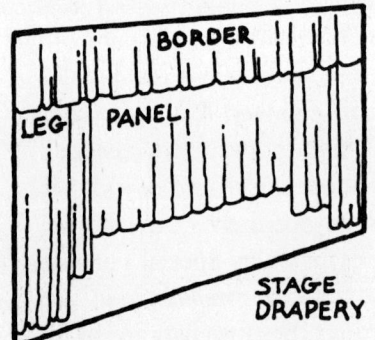

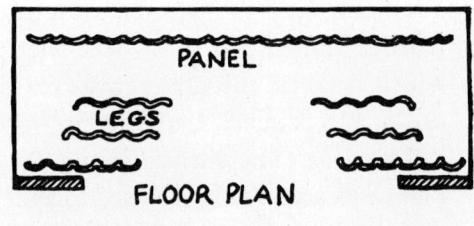

A *drop* is a piece of fabric (usually of canvas or muslin) on which a scene is painted. Some drops are cut as well as painted. All drops are hung from overhead battens and are weighted at the bottom with a batten or a chain so they will hang straight and move as little as possible. There are various types of drops.

■ The *plain drop*—a solid piece of fabric, often as large as the proscenium opening. When it serves as background to a scene, it is called a *backdrop.*

■ The *cut drop*—a plain drop with a hole or holes cut in it; the audience sees the actors performing through the "holes" as if through a frame. Trees, columns, or other appropriate scenery are painted around the opening. The part of the drop which touches the floor is not cut.

■ The *leg drop*—a drop with a large central section—including the part which would touch the floor—cut out of it, so that its basic shape is something like that of an upsidedown U.

- The *cut border*—a short, teaser-like drop which is cut irregularly along the lower edge. When leaves are painted on it, it is called a *foliage border*.
- The *leg*—a narrow, long drop, like a single drapery leg, but, like all drops, painted and more solid in appearance than a drape.

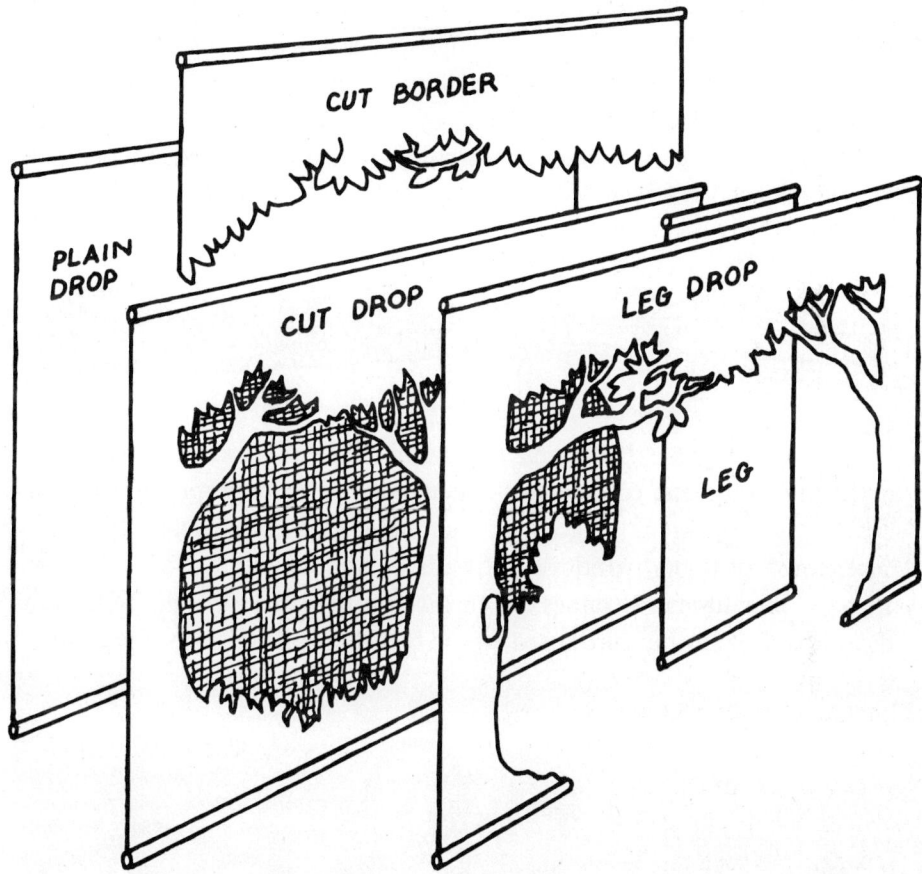

A *scrim* is another type of drop. It is made of a loosely woven fabric that resembles cheesecloth. A scrim becomes transparent when there is properly directed light behind it. When light is directed onto a scrim from the front, the scrim becomes opaque, hiding everything behind it. If a scene is painted on the front of a scrim, it will *appear* when the light hits it from the front, and *disappear* when those lights are faded out and the rear lighting is brought up.

The *cyclorama* or *cyc* is a large single piece of material which hangs from a (usually) curved pipe batten and forms a background for a stage setting. While its main function is to represent sky or "endless space" (a void), it is sometimes painted with a scene for certain shows.

A *wing* is a rectangular scenery unit resembling a plain flat. Fabric is stretched over a wooden or metal frame and painted with a design. Wings are placed as legs are, at the sides of the stage to mask the backstage area. (See page 136 for the use of wings in a drop-and-wing setting.)

A *ground row* is a long, low piece of scenery which stands on the stage floor and represents a low strip of rocks, bushes, hills, or the like. Ground rows are constructed of narrow jogs which are shaped and painted to give the needed effect.

The *frame* is a useful scenic unit when financial resources are limited or when a complete, realistic set is not required or appropriate. Frames can be used on arena stages, because instead of being solid, they are "skeletons" of doors, windows, or walls. They are built of 1″ × 2″ or 1″ × 3″ pine lumber. Frames can be given further detail, if desired, with the addition of cut-out cardboard, upson board, masonite, or thin plywood.

The *screen* is a solid rectangular structure with a base which allows it to stand up on its own—like decorative screens sold in antique stores. They are excellent substitutes for flats, and can be useful for low-budget shows with little scenery. A frequently used size is four feet wide by eight feet high. Screens can be placed in various arrangements onstage or even in the classroom to establish walls and entrances. If they aren't antiques, and if the person who owns them agrees, you can paint or decorate them to suit your particular production—or paint them a neutral color so you can use them for any production.

Projections can provide interesting scenic effects. With them, designers and technicians can create shadows, silhouetted lines and shapes—even color scenes.

In school productions, most projections are done from the front, from somewhere in the house. Standard school equipment, like the ordinary slide or overhead projector, is used.

In professional productions, projections are often done from the rear of the stage, behind the playing area. This means no one has to worry about shadows thrown by moving actors. With professional equipment also, special effects—drifting clouds, waves, falling snow or rain—are possible.

The screen used for projections from the front can be any flat surface which is white or a solid light color. The back wall of your stage might serve as a screen. A connected group of plain flats or a plain backdrop could also serve the purpose.

STANDARD SETS

The *box set*—A great many plays require an *interior* setting, such as a living room, an office, a kitchen, a throne room, or a dungeon. Such an interior is often indicated by means of a box set consisting basically of two or more walls made of flats usually as high as or higher than the proscenium arch. Box sets often have actual ceilings. While the word *box* suggests a square or rectangle, your designer will probably improvise on that idea by varying the straight lines of the walls to make the set more interesting.

☐ Examine the following floor plans of box sets. Explain to the class how you would change them to suit an interior for a play you have read. (You may want to explain the play briefly.) Draw your idea on the blackboard.

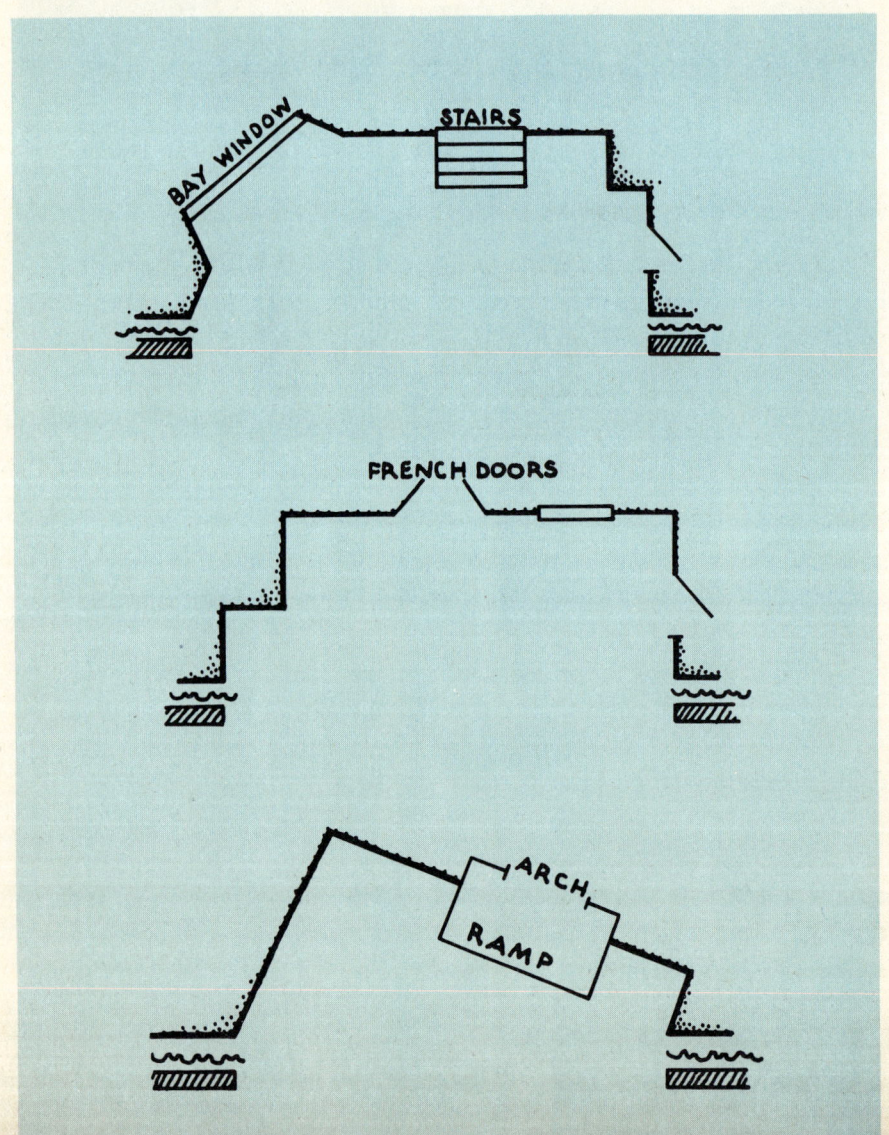

The *exterior set*—If a play is set outdoors—in an alley, a ranch corral, the front of a tenement building—it needs an exterior set. Flats, ground rows, and drops, plus raised platforms, plywood trees, papier-mâché rocks, and whatever else is appropriate are combined to represent the desired locale.

☐ Find a play that requires at least one exterior set. Imagine that you are going to direct it and, using the following drawings as examples, sketch a design for the set you would suggest to the designer. Show the drawing to your drama group and explain, from your point of view as a director, how it would enrich the production.

The *drop-and-wing set* or *wing-and-border set*—Interiors and exteriors for productions in which realism is not especially important are sometimes created by an arrangement of painted drops, cut borders, and wings.

The *unit set*—A unit set is made up of large sturdy pieces—ramps, steps, platforms—which can be arranged on a bare stage to suit each scene of a play. The advantage of this kind of set is that the crew can simply rearrange the same pieces of scenery whenever the scene shifts to a different locale.

The *minimal* or *fragmentary set*—Most audiences are quite willing to use their imaginations to fill in the missing pieces. They will usually accept a set that effectively combines a few flats, screens, or frames with stage draperies and props.

Sets, as we've said before, don't have to be elaborate—or even complete—to be effective. A bare stage with a little furniture and effective lighting can communicate the right feeling of solemnity for a tragedy or drama. A comedy can be just as funny played in front of a few carefully placed colorful screens as it can when played in a full box set. Frames, perhaps with abstract cutouts, can enhance the flavor of a fantasy. Don't be alarmed if your school doesn't have a complete collection of flats and other basic equipment. All you really need is an imaginative and ingenious designer!

STAGE PROPERTIES

We've already talked a little about *hand props*—the small items you carry onstage or handle as an actor. Hand props can be swords, canes, glasses, food, teapots, needle and thread, fire pokers. But there are other kinds of props as well. In general, anything which is not part of the architecture of the set—anything that is not a wall, platform, ramp, step unit, stage drape, or drop—is a prop. There are three kinds of props, in addition to hand props.

Set props or *scene props*—These are large items which are placed on the floor—mostly furniture, rugs, statuary, small rocks or bushes, tree stumps, garden furniture. Lamps, candlesticks, piles of magazines, and similar items placed *on* the furniture are also set props.

Dress or *trim props*—Dress or trim props are used to decorate (or dress up) the walls of the set. They include pictures, window curtains, plaques, wall torches, etc.

Effects props—In many productions, special effects like crashes, doorbells, smoke, fire, wind, and fog are the responsibility of the property crew. You'll notice many of those effects involve sound. When sound effects are recorded, they are usually handled by the sound crew instead of the prop crew.

A special word about props—Many props—even large set props—are borrowed for the show by the prop crew. Sometimes props are the treasured property of members of the cast or their relatives; sometimes they are valuable items borrowed from stores. All borrowed props, of course, must be returned in perfect condition—and therefore should be handled with care by actors as well as by the prop crew. If you damage or lose a prop, notify the prop crew right away!

STAGE LIGHTING

The major functions of lighting are (1) to *illuminate* the actors, the set, and the action, so the audience can see them, (2) to indicate *time and weather* (night or day, winter or summer, a sunny or cloudy day) and to indicate changes in time and weather, (3) to set a *mood*—happy, tragic, sombre.

Most standard stage lighting equipment falls into two categories: general and specific. General lighting instruments spread light very broadly over large areas of scenery and over a sizeable portion of the acting area. Specific lighting instruments emit relatively narrow beams of light. Individually, they illuminate small areas. But they are frequently used in groups to light the main acting area.

Lighting equipment, especially control equipment, has changed a great deal in the last ten to fifteen years. Many schools have some of the most modern equipment—plus some of the oldest. Many professional theaters do also. To make matters even more confusing, the terminology used in lighting, even more than in scenery construction, is apt to vary. What I call a Leko, for example, you may call a Klieglite—or simply a spot. We've tried to list here the most commonly used names for the most basic and standard instruments—but you may hear other names used, and see instruments not mentioned here.

General Lighting Instruments

Borderlights or *striplights* consist of a collection of lamps (light bulbs) placed in an open trough or in individual compartments within a trough. They are usually hung from pipe battens above the acting area. Sometimes they are placed on the floor to light the bottom of a cyc or drop, in which case they are sometimes called *cyc foots*.

Footlights are similar, but they are placed on the apron of the stage, aimed so they throw light upwards. In some theaters, they are built into the apron and can be made to disappear into the stage floor.

Floodlights are large instruments, consisting of a single high wattage lamp placed in a simple frame. They are designed to spread as much light as possible over a wide area. The most common kinds of floods are the *scoop* (in a round frame) and the *Olivette* (in a square frame). Both kinds can be hung from battens or mounted on stands; both are used to light walls, cycs, and backings—flats or drops placed behind openings such as windows or doors. They are both also used to provide a strong concentration of light through a window, from a hall, or a like area.

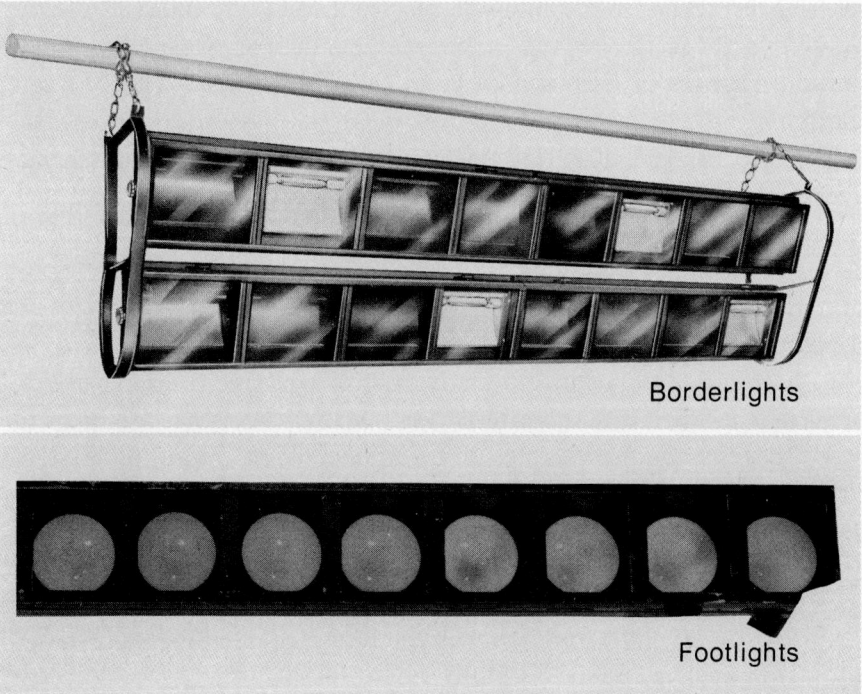

Borderlights

Footlights

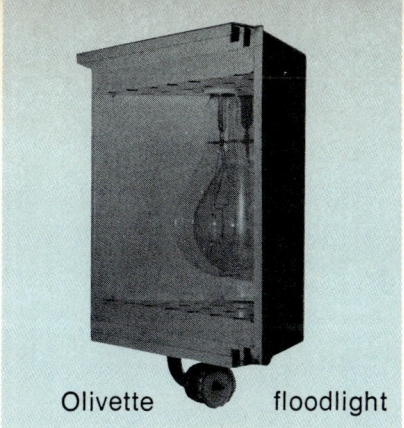
Olivette floodlight

Specific Lighting Instruments

The instruments in this group are spotlights. Most spots have three basic parts—a lamp, a reflector, and a lens. Spots can be focused to direct a strong beam of light on a particular area of the stage or set. Some standard spots are named for the lenses they use.

The *plano-convex (P.C.) spotlight* has a lens that is flat on one side and curved on the other. It uses a lamp from 500 to 2,000 watts. P.C.s are usually hung from the "first pipe" (the overhead pipe batten closest to the proscenium arch), or from the front of the balcony. They may also be directed toward the stage from the projection booth, or from the sides of the house. Because of the nature of the lens, the beam of light from a P.C. is sharp and clearly defined.

The *baby spot* also contains a plano-convex lens, but it uses a lower wattage lamp—usually between 100 and 400 watts. Baby spots are best hung from the first pipe or used to illuminate backings.

The *Fresnel spotlight* is also named for its lens, which has the special feature of softening the edges of the beam of light thrown through it. Fresnels use lamps ranging from 500 to 3,000 watts. They are most effective when mounted on pipes in groups to light the acting area or used to illuminate backings.

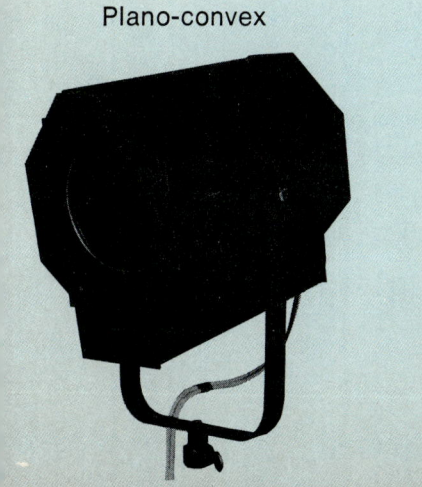
Plano-convex

Baby spotlight

Fresnel spotlight

Ellipsoidal spotlight

Follow spotlight

The *ellipsoidal spot* gets its name not from the lens it uses, but from the shape of the reflector behind the lamp. However, these spots are often called by their brand names as well—Leko, Klieglite. Small ellipsoidals usually use one or two plano-convex lenses and 250 or 500 watt lamps. Larger units use 750 to 3,000 watt lamps and a single lens called a step lens. Because they can throw a powerful beam, ellipsoidals are best mounted in the ceiling of the house, at the sides of the house, or on the front of the balcony or the projection booth. They are generally used in groups to light the downstage acting areas.

The *follow spot* is usually the largest and highest wattage instrument used. It throws a strong beam on a selected place or actor on the stage, and can be swiveled by its operator to follow a particular action. The size and color of the beam can also be controlled by the operator. Follow spots are run from the back of the house or from the projection booth.

The *beam projector* or *lensless spotlight,* as its name suggests, has no lens. However, because of its powerful lamp and efficient reflector, it can throw an intense, narrow beam of light—good for sunlight and moonlight effects.

The Lighting Control System

Theatrical lighting is controlled at a central switchboard or control board. Each lighting instrument or group of instruments is plugged into this board. The electrician assigned to the board can turn lights, singly or in groups, on or off or make them brighter or dimmer by operating the controls. Some modern control systems are extremely sophisticated. The electronic age has made its way backstage. There are boards available today which feature tubes, printed circuits, memory banks, and can be programmed in much the same way that computers are. On cue, the stage electrician might press a single button or drop a pre-coded card in a slot, and then sit back while a complex, prearranged light change occurs.

COLOR IN LIGHTING

A pure white light is seldom used on stage because it tends to be glaring and harsh. Except for some borderlights or footlights in which colored lamps are used, colored light onstage is usually achieved by placing a colored but translucent sheet in front of each instrument. The materials used for these sheets are geletine (gel), or a plastic color medium marketed under the brand names Roscolene, Cinebex, and Cinemoid.

Every lighting instrument, when it is new, comes with a gel (or color) frame. The gel (or Roscolene, or whatever) is cut to fit this frame and placed into slots on the front of the flood, spot, or borderlight.

BACKSTAGE ORGANIZATION

You as actor or director have worked hard through a long rehearsal period to get ready for opening night. While you've been rehearsing, the designers and technicians have been working on the set, the props, the lighting, the sound, and the costumes. Before that first curtain goes up, you will take part in a number of rehearsals with the technicians. The backstage crews are as essential to a smooth performance as you are—and as are the "front of the house crews" (ushers, box office person, ticket takers, publicity people). Your show will go more smoothly if you know what each of your backstage colleagues is responsible for.

Your drama group probably won't have a separate person assigned to every job noted in the chart below. The ideal technical staff, however, looks like this:

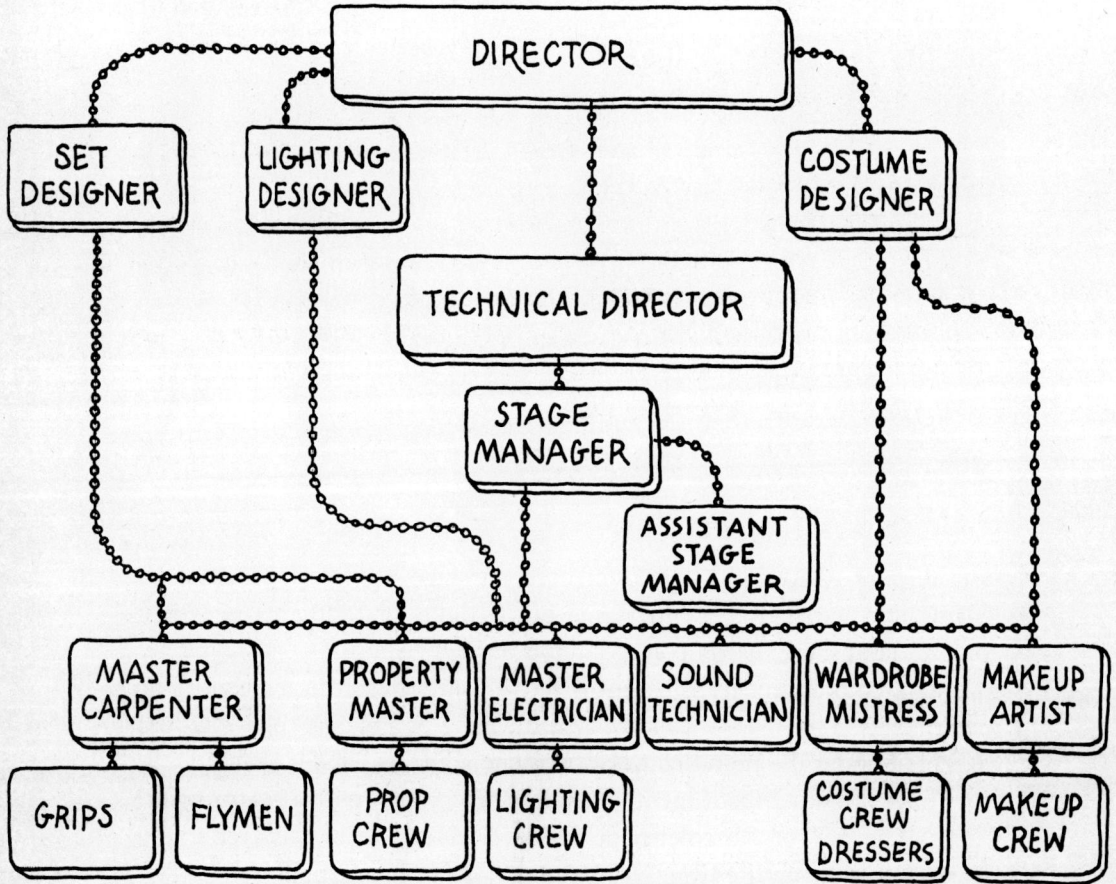

Job Descriptions

The *technical director* oversees the building, painting, and assembling of all the technical ingredients of the show; with the stage manager, he or she selects and trains the crews who will run the show through rehearsals and performances.

The *stage manager* is the actual working foreman of the entire backstage crew.

The *assistant stage manager* does chores for the s.m.; prompts the actors during rehearsals and performances if they forget their lines.

The *master carpenter* is in charge of the crew that sets and shifts the scenery. The master electrician is in charge of the crew which operates the lighting control board, follow spots, projectors, and all other electrical equipment.

The *property master* or *mistress* is in charge of the crew which obtains all props and places and shifts them onstage and backstage. This crew head also supervises sound effects in some cases, and takes care of the general housekeeping of the stage set (dusting, sweeping the stage, etc.).

The *sound technician* operates the sound system when recorded sound effects or incidental music are required.

The *wardrobe mistress* or *master* supervises the collecting, cleaning, pressing, repair, and distribution of costumes; the crew may include *dressers* who help actors to make difficult or quick changes.

The *makeup artist* supervises the crew that applies makeup to the actors in situations in which the actors do not do this themselves and keeps all the theater's cosmetics clean, neat, and in good supply.

SUMMING UP

Wherever you do plays, some form of scenery is usually provided and maneuvered by a backstage crew. The stage set they make will help to emphasize and establish the characters, mood, time, and place of the play. Those four ideas may be communicated literally—with complete sets which represent places realistically—or they may be *suggested*—figuratively and simply—by a few well-chosen scenery and prop pieces.

The costumes and makeup *and* the crafts-people responsible for them give you as an actor or director external but personal aids which help you develop a complete and unified production. The sets, props, lighting, and sound, *and* the designers and technicians in charge of them provide the actors' onstage environment.

When we say it is your responsibility to know all you can about theatrical production—including the technical elements—we are not setting up a mere exercise in *appreciation* of the machinery of the theater and of the backstage personnel in charge of it. You should *know* as much as you can about production, because a well-informed, well-rehearsed, well-coordinated alliance of director, designer, cast, crew, and "front of house" people has the best chance of producing the hit of the season.

The *appreciation* comes from the audience. (Applause!)

Activities

☐ Select one of the subjects listed below. Then consult your school or local library and list the titles and authors of all the books you find which deal with the subject you chose.

    a. stage scenery design
    b. stage scenery construction
    c. stage scenery painting
    d. the use of projections in stage sets
    e. stage lighting design
    f. stage lighting equipment
    g. stage properties
    h. sound effects
    i. costume design and construction
    j. stage makeup (straight)
    k. stage makeup (old age)
    l. stage makeup (character)
    m. duties of the stage manager
    n. duties of stage crews
        (1) carpenters
        (2) property crew
        (3) electricians
        (4) sound technicians

        (5)   costume people
        (6)   makeup people
  o. Duties of "front of the house" crews
        (1)   house manager and ushers
        (2)   box office people
        (3)   publicity people

☐ Share the titles of the tech books you found with the members of your drama group. Cooperate in making a composite index which will be available to the class for study projects and for use when information is needed for preparing the technical aspects of plays.

☐ Cooperate with your group in making a list of the supply houses nearest you which sell materials and equipment necessary for stage productions. Use these sources: books on play production and tech theater, the classified section of city telephone directories, theater teachers assigned to your school or to nearby schools and colleges, employees and members of local community theater groups. Write each company for a catalog and price list and make these part of your group's informational resources.

CURTAIN TIME: A PERFORMANCE CHECKLIST

FOR THE DIRECTOR

Because of your careful planning, casting, staffing, and rehearsing of the production, your responsibilities on performance days should be few. (Exception: in some school productions, the director pulls the curtain, gives cues, and in general runs the show from backstage. But it may be easier on both you and the cast if you don't do this—unless there's no one else who can.) You will, however, probably want to make a few last-minute checks before curtain time.

- Check with the stage manager (or whoever is in charge backstage) to learn if every member of the cast and crew is there and ready. (Be available to answer questions and for emergencies, but—in general—leave them alone to complete their jobs as they rehearsed them.)
- Check to make sure the front-of-the-house people (house manager, ushers, and box office staff) are ready.
- Go backstage about ten minutes before curtain time and give a short pep talk to the cast and crew. Keep your remarks calm, but peppy and cheerful. Don't give notes; instead, express your confidence in the entire production team. If the audience out front is large and seems responsive and ready to enjoy the show, tell the cast and crew.
- Give the stage manager or whoever is in charge the okay to call "Places!" and start the show.
- Take your place *in the audience* (notebook and pen in hand if you want to take notes), and . . .
- Enjoy the show!

FOR THE ACTOR

You're excited! The show is about to begin! Perhaps you have "butterflies" in your stomach; if you don't you're not very typical—MOST performers feel some degree of anxiousness—nervousness—before going on. But that's normal, even useful when you direct that excess energy toward your role. Here are some hints on how to be as calm as possible and how to make sure you're alert and ready to perform when the moment comes.

- Get a lot of rest before each performance.
- Refresh and relax yourself with a shower or bath.
- Report to the theater at least forty-five minutes before curtain time (sooner, if the stage manager or director announces an earlier call).
- If you haven't left your valuables at home (a good idea), check them with the stage manager or with a friend who will not be on the stage.
- Spend your time backstage putting yourself in the mood and spirit of the play. Save kidding around for *after* the performance.
- Check to see that your costume is clean, pressed, and all there.
- Put on your costume. Walk around in the dressing room area to make sure you feel free and comfortable in it.
- Check your makeup. Is the back of your neck covered, your ears, your hands if necessary, and all exposed skin? Does it match the makeup job which was approved by the director during dress rehearsal?
- Check your general appearance in a mirror.
- See if your personal props for Act One are on the prop table (check props for later acts as they occur). *DO NOT* walk away with any of your props, however—the stage manager or prop person will be checking them too. Pick them up only moments before you enter.
- Spend a few minutes doing gentle "calisthenics"—rolling your head, yawning, shaking your hands and wrists vigorously, bobbing loosely from the waist to touch your toes. These exercises should help you relax and make your body feel alive.
- When you hear the call "Places!" pick up your hand props and immediately take your place in the wings (or onstage, or wherever you are supposed to be).
- Just before going on, get *into character*, totally. Forget your personal worries and concentrate on your role. *Become* the whole character you developed in rehearsals.
- Listen for your cue.
- Enter *in character*.
- *Break a leg!* (Actor talk for "Good Luck!")

BOOKS TO READ

GENERAL

An Introduction to the Theatre, by Frank M. Whiting. 3rd edition. New York: Harper & Row, 1969. (The literature, arts, and crafts of the drama in terms of how plays have been acted and produced throughout history.)

Invitation to the Theatre, by George R. Kernodle. New York: Harcourt Brace Jovanovich, 1967. (Introductory textbook; gives a broad view of all the major forms of theater art.)

The Living Stage: A History of the World Theatre, by Kenneth Macgowan and W. Melnitz. Englewood Cliffs, N.J.: Prentice-Hall, 1955. (Illustrated study of theaters, plays, acting, directing, and staging.)

On Stage: A History of the Theatre, by Vera Mowry Roberts. 3rd edition. New York: Harper & Row, 1974. (Comprehensive book; looks at theater—actors, directors, designers, playwrights, and audiences—in the social framework.)

A Primer for Playgoers: An Introduction to the Understanding and Appreciation of Cinema-Stage-Television, by Edward A. Wright. Englewood Cliffs, N.J.: Prentice-Hall, 1958. (Includes a glossary of theatrical terms and questions for discussion groups.)

The Story of America's Musical Theatre, by David Ewen. Philadelphia: Chilton, 1968. (Starts with the first known American musical show—1735.)

Teach Yourself Guidebook to the Drama, by Luis Vargas. New York: Dover, 1961. (Brief treatment of the development of drama in the Western world.)

The Theatre: An Introduction, by Oscar G. Brockett. 3rd edition. New York: Holt, Rinehart and Winston, 1974. (Survey of Western dramatic literature, using professional theater standards.)

A Theatre in Your Head: Analyzing Its Production, by Kenneth Thorpe Rowe. New York: Funk & Wagnalls, 1970. (A study of the structure of a written playscript; criteria for visualizing an ideal production.)

ACTING

Acting Is Believing, by Charles J. McGraw. 2nd edition. New York: Holt, Rinehart and Winston, 1966. (A book for the beginning actor based on selected aspects of the Stanislavski method of acting; emphasizes what an actor does physically and mentally to fully develop a characterization.)

Acting: The First Six Lessons, by Richard Boleslavsky. New York: Theatre Arts Books, 1933. (This director of the Moscow Art Theater discusses concentration, emotion memory, dramatic action, characterization, observation, and rhythm.)

The Actor at Work, by Robert L. Benedetti. Englewood Cliffs, N.J.: Prentice-Hall, 1970. (Features exercises in total use of the body for freeing the actor from inhibitions.)

An Actor Prepares, by Constantin Stanislavsky. New York: Theatre Arts Books, 1946. (The basic handbook of the Stanislavski method of acting. Two others, also by Stanislavski, are *Building a Character* and *Creating a Role.* Both are published by Threatre Arts Books.)

The Composite Art of Acting, by Jerry Blunt. New York: Macmillan, 1966. (A study of acting theory and technique; includes practice scenes.)

The Craftsmen of Dionysus: An Approach to Acting, by Jerome Rockwood. Glenview, Ill.: Scott, Foresman, 1966. (Psychological and physical preparation are described as important tasks of the actor; the book includes sections on characterization, role analysis, and acting in period plays.)

First Steps in Acting, by Samuel Selden and Hubert Heffner. 2nd edition. New York: Appleton-Century-Crofts, 1964. (Emphasizes stage imagery, language, pantomime, and vocal technique; has practice scenes and glossary.)

The Magic If: Stanislavsky for Children, by Elizabeth Y. Kelly. Baltimore: National Education Press, 1973. (A simplified explanation of the Stanislavski method of acting.)

Speech for the Stage, by Evangeline Machlin. New York: Theatre Arts Books, 1967. (A book about speech written directly to the young actor.)

The Technique of Acting, by Francis C. Strickland. New York: McGraw-Hill, 1956. (Has exercises for developing a young actor's complete technique of dramatic expression, including phrasing, building a dramatic climax, action, timing, pointing, rhythm, pace, and style.)

To the Actor, by Michael Chekov. New York: Harper & Row, 1953. (Contains worthwhile exercises on body, psychology, imagination, improvisation, and characterization.)

Working Up a Part, by Harry D. Albright. 2nd edition. Boston: Houghton Mifflin, 1959. (This manual considers analyzing and rehearsing a part in the areas of movement, interpretation, voice and articulation, characterization; the appendix includes "a primer of stage directing for the beginning actor.")

DIRECTING

Amateur Theatre: A Guide for Actor and Director, by Van H. D. Cartmell. New York: Funk & Wagnall, 1968. (A beginning director's handbook; includes a complete working script.)

The Director in the Theatre, by Marian Gallaway. New York: Macmillan, 1963. (A comprehensive workbook dealing with the role of the director at various points in the production process.)

Fundamentals of Play Directing, by Alexander Dean and Lawrence Carra. 3rd edition. New York: Holt, Rinehart and Winston, 1973. (On directing for the proscenium, arena, thrust and flexible stages; a revision of the earlier work of the late Professor Dean of the Yale School of Drama.)

MAKEUP

Stage Make-Up, by Richard Corson. 4th edition. New York: Appleton-Century-Crofts, 1967. (Complete guide, including instructions and color illustrations.)

Stage Makeup, by Herman Buchman. New York: Watson-Guptill Publications, 1971. (Fully illustrated; some color.)

COSTUME

Dressing the Part: A History of Costume for the Theatre, by Fairfax P. Walkup. Revised edition. New York: Appleton-Century-Crofts, 1950. (Illustrated, comprehensive study of period dress and its application to stage costuming.)

Historic Costume for the Stage, by Lucy R. Barton. Revised edition. Boston: Baker's Plays, 1961. (Covers period costume from Egypt to early 20th century; pattern- and costume-making are included.)

The Mode in Costume, by R. Turner Wilcox. New York: Scribner's, 1969. (1300 full-figure drawings with appropriate notes on the major periods of dress.)

Stage Costume Handbook, by Berneice Prisk. New York: Harper & Row, 1966. (Treats design and construction, as well as dress, through periods of history.)

SCENERY AND LIGHTING

Essentials of Stage Lighting, by Hunton D. Sellman. New York: Appleton-Century-Crofts, 1972. (A complete book on design and practice; includes information about and illustrations of modern lighting and projection equipment.)

Here's How: A Guide to Economy in Stagecraft, by Herbert V. Hake. New York: Samuel French, 1958. (Step-by-step illustrated instructions for set building and painting, and for lighting; budgeting is stressed.)

Lighting the Stage: Art and Practice, by Willard F. Bellman. New York: Chandler, 1974. (Complete book of lighting design; includes sections on electrical safety and the latest in electronic control boards.)

A Method of Lighting the Stage, by Stanley McCandless. New York: Theatre Arts Books, 1954. (The author's theories of lighting design; long considered a standard basic book in the field.)

Stagecraft and Scene Design, by Herbert Philippi. Boston: Houghton Mifflin, 1953. (This illustrated book treats the design, construction, rigging, handling, and lighting of stage scenery.)

Stage Scenery: Its Construction and Rigging, by Arnold S. Gillette and J. Jeffrey Auer. 2nd edition. New York: Harper & Row, 1972. (Illustrated instructional manual for technical staff and designer.)

Theatrical Lighting Practice, by Joel E. Rubin and Leland H. Watson. New York: Theatre Arts Books, 1954. (Handbook that covers proscenium and arena staging, television, puppet shows.)

Play Production

A Stage Crew Handbook, by Sol Cornberg and Emanuel Gebauer. 4th edition. New York: Harper & Row, 1957. (Stagecraft book for the scene designer, technical director, stage manager, set builders and painters, and property master or mistress; includes many detailed illustrations.)

The Stage Manager's Handbook, by Bert Gruver. Revised edition. New York: DBS Publications, 1972. (Complete book for the entire backstage crew; includes a model of a stage manager's prompt script.)

Theatre Backstage from A to Z, by Warren C. Lounsbury. Revised edition. Seattle: University of Washington Press, 1972. (Heavily illustrated glossary of technical stage terms.)

Play Catalogs

These are best obtained by writing directly to the publishing companies. Some of the best-known:
Walter H. Baker Co., 100 Summer St., Boston, MA 02128.
Dramatic Publishing Co., 179 North Michigan Ave., Chicago, IL 60601.
Dramatists Play Service, 14 East 38th St., New York, NY 10016
Samuel French, Inc., 25 West 45th St., New York, NY 10036; or, 7623 Sunset Boulevard, Hollywood, CA 90046.

Glossary of Terms

Not all the terms in the following list are used in this book. But they are all terms you may hear at one time or another around any theater. We have not repeated in this glossary the terminology covered in Chapter 8 for the parts of the theater, for scenery units, for sets, for stage properties, and for lighting equipment. These terms are all listed in the index, however, so you can refer to them quickly if necessary.

acoustics: the qualities of a room (or other space) that make it easy or difficult to hear distinctly.

ad-lib: to improvise something (usually dialogue) which is not in the script and has not been rehearsed.

aside: a character's lines spoken directly to the audience, presumably out of earshot of other characters in the play.

audition: try-out; a trial reading or performance designed to determine an actor's suitability for a role in a play.

backing: a piece of scenery placed behind windows, doors, and other openings in the walls of a set to hide the backstage area from the audience.

backstage: all areas of a theater behind the house curtain.

batten: a strip of wood or length of pipe from which scenery or lighting is hung; also used to stiffen unframed scenery such as backdrops and cycs.

bit part: a small role in a play.

black light: ultraviolet light; a light which causes certain colors and materials to glow in the dark.

blackout: total darkness onstage—achieved by pulling the main switch or the master (main) dimmer.

blacks: black-dyed stage draperies.

blocking: the planned movements (traffic pattern) of actors onstage.

business (stage): actions such as gestures, serving refreshments, playing checkers, etc. (but not including movement from point to point onstage) done by an actor in a play.

call board: the bulletin board upon which rehearsal schedules, crew schedules, and general notices are posted.

character part: a role in a play which is quite different from an actor's normal personality, often used to refer to elderly characters, funny characters, etc.

chorus: performers who dance, sing, or speak as a group.

"clear": a backstage command used for signaling actors or crew members to get out of the way or to remove scenery, props, etc.

climax: a moment in a play of high dramatic interest, when the action that has been building reaches its high point.

commedia dell'arte: an improvised comic acting style popular in sixteenth through eighteenth century Italy.

conflict: the problem or struggle faced by the main character in a play.

contour curtain: a house curtain that can be raised to form a scalloped or other irregular shape within the proscenium opening.

cross: a stage direction to an actor meaning "walk" or "move" from one part of the stage to another; the action of crossing.

cue: a signal (spoken or written) that prompts a cast or crew member to respond with a particular line or action.

cue sheet: a list of directions used to remind stage managers and crewheads when and how to execute light changes, scenery shifts, etc.

curtain line: an imaginary line which marks the position of a closed house curtain; also, the final line of an act or a scene which serves as a cue to close the house curtain.

deck: the stage floor.

denouement: the final disentangling, unravelling, solution of the problem or intricacies of the plot of a play.

dialogue: the lines spoken by characters in a play.

diction: the choice and enunciation of words, especially with regard to correctness, clarity, and effectiveness.

dimmer: a device (part of the switchboard) for changing the intensity of stage lighting.

doubling: an actor's portraying more than one role in a single play.

dress rehearsal: a nonstop rehearsal (except for act and scene breaks)—with complete sets, costumes, makeup, etc.—held shortly before opening night.

elevation: a platform or ramp used as part of a stage set; also, a flat mechanical drawing showing dimensions and details of scenery units of a stage set as viewed from eye level.

entrance: any opening in the scenery through which an actor can enter onto the playing area; also, the action of entering.

epilogue: a speech (often in verse) spoken directly to the audience after the end of a play.

false proscenium: a frame (placed upstage of the house curtain) to cut down the size of the proscenium opening.

flies: the space above the stage from which scenery is hung.

floor cloth: (see **ground cloth**).

floor plan: ground plan; a drawing (usually in scale) showing the layout of scenery and set props on the stage floor.

fourth wall: the imaginary, invisible "wall" through which an audience watches a play (usually used in connection with a realistic set on a proscenium stage).

green room: a backstage room in which actors and crew wait for their entrance cues or wait to report for assigned duties (the talk given to a cast by the director immediately prior to a performance is sometimes called a "green room").

grip: a stagehand (on the carpenter's crew) whose job is to set and strike (remove) all standing scenery (walls, platforms, ramps, etc.).

ground cloth: floor cloth; a canvas cloth used to cover the acting area; helps to tone down noise and glare of the stage floor; can be painted to blend with the set.

ground plan: (see **floor plan**).

hand properties: small items carried onstage or handled by an actor in a play (fans, canes, teacups, coins).

house lights: lights which illuminate the audience seating area of a theater or auditorium.

improvisation: an original, spontaneous scene or other theatrical piece created by actors without benefit of a script.

ingenue: a naive or innocent girl or young woman in a play; also, the actress playing such a role.

juvenile: a boy or young man in a play; also, the actor playing such a role.

leading man/leading woman (or lady): the actor or actress in the principal role in a play.

lens: a specially designed piece of glass or plastic used to change (usually by concentrating) rays of light passing through; lenses are used on most spotlights.

loft: the space above the gridiron but below the ceiling of the stage house.

masking: scenery units used to hide backstage areas from the audience.

monologue (see **soliloquy**): a dramatic piece written for one actor or performed by one actor; also, a long speech in a play spoken by one actor.

objective: the goal of a character in a given unit of a play or in the entire play.

pace: the tempo or speed at which a production moves during performance.

parallel: (see **platform**).

perspective: a drawing that gives the illusion of depth and distance to the items depicted.

"places": a command for alerting actors and crew to go to an assigned place and be ready to start the scene or execute their responsibilities.

platform: riser; a raised, movable structure on which actors may perform and to which sets may be attached; if it is collapsible, it is called a *parallel*.

prompt book: the stage manager's copy of the playscript, complete with blocking and technical cues.

properties: all items which are not part of the architecture of a set—*set* or *scene props:* furniture, rugs, etc.; *dress* or *trim props:* pictures, window curtains, etc.; *effects props:* doorbells, thunder, etc.; also, see **hand properties.**

proscenium arch: the "picture frame" through which an audience watches the action of a play in a proscenium theater.

realism: a dramatic form that attempts to reproduce nature and people truthfully and faithfully (as in real life).

repertory theater: a production of a theatrical company which presents several plays successively (or alternately) in the same season.

reversal: a point in a play when the action changes from the direction in which it appeared to be going.

right stage: (see **stage right**).

roll curtain: a stage curtain which is raised and lowered much as a window shade is.

running: a method of shifting scenery by sliding it along the stage floor.

run-through: a play rehearsal in which an entire scene, act, or play is done without interruptions.

scenario: an outline of the plot of a play, giving particulars of characters, scenes, and situations.

scene: a division of an act or a play generally determined by a lapse of time, a change of locale, or the entrance of a major character.

scene dock: a backstage area for storing scenery.

script: playscript; an acting edition of a play.

set: setting; the background or scenery used in the staging of a play.

sides: a partial script containing only one actor's lines and the cues to those lines.

sight lines: the lines of vision from any seat in the house to any part of the stage.

soliloquy: a speech from a play wherein the actor, usually alone onstage, speaks to him- or herself.

stage crew: all persons who work backstage on the technical elements of a production.

stage left: the left one-third of the stage as the actor faces the audience.

stage right: the right one-third of the stage as the actor faces the audience.

strike: a backstage term for removing all or part of the set from the stage.

tableau: a static scene composed of actors who do not move.

technical rehearsal: a rehearsal in which scene shifts, lights, sound, costumes, etc., are practiced and/or checked.

upstaging: when an actor moves to an upstage position, thereby forcing other actors to speak lines with their backs to the audience.

wagon (see **platform**): a low platform on wheels or casters upon which parts of a stage set may be erected for quick or easy scene changes.

working drawings: detailed diagrams drawn to scale (specifications) from which scenery is built.

Index

Acoustics, 42
Act curtain, 125
Acting
   during rehearsals, 115-120
   improvisation and, 61-65
   training for, 47-59
Adaptations, 19-25
Apron, 125
Arena stage, 36, 37, 39, 95, 127
Asbestos curtain, 125
Auditions, 10-15, 89
Auditorium, 33-34, 124-126

Balcony, 125, 126
Baby spot, 139
Backdrop, 130
Battens, 130
Beam projector, 140
Blocking, 91-96
Blocking rehearsal, 105-108, 117-118
Border, 130, 131, 136
Borderlights, 138
Box set, 133-134, 136
Business, stage, 106, 117

Casting
  how to cast, 10-15, 88-89
  standards for, 5-7, 13-14
Chamber theater, 22-24
Characterization, 74-81
Characterization rehearsal, 108-110
Cinebex, 141
Cinemoid, 141
Curtain calls, 114-115
Curtains, stage, 125, 126
Cut border, 131, 136
Cut drop, 130
Cyclorama (cyc), 132
Cyc foots, 138

Directing
  pre-rehearsal work, 86-96
  during rehearsals, 99-115
  improvisational approach to, 109, 111-112
Door flat, 129

Drapes, 130, 131, 132, 136
Draw curtain, 125
Dress rehearsal, 113-114, 119-120
Drop, 130-131, 136
Drop-and-wing set, 136
Drop curtain, 125

Ellipsoidal spot, 140
Exterior set, 135

Fire curtain, 125
Fireplace flat, 129
Flats, 129
Floodlights, 138
Floor plan, 90, 105-106
Follow spot, 140
Footlights, 138
Forestage, 125
Fragmentary set, 136
Frame, 132, 136
Fresnel spotlight, 139

Gel, 141
Grand drape, 125
Grand valence, 125
Ground row, 132

House, 124-125, 126
House curtain, 125

Improvisation
  for actor training, 61-65
  for auditions, 11-12, 89
  creating productions through, 25-30
  directing, 86-87, 91, 111-112
  in rehearsals, 109
Interior setting, 133

Jackknife curtain, 125
Jog, 129, 132

Klieglite, 137, 140

L-shaped theater, 38
Leg, 131

157

Leg drop, 130
Legs, 130
Leko, 137, 140
Lensless spotlight, 140
Light booth, 125
Lighting, stage, 137–141
Loge, 125

Mansion stage, 40
Minimal set, 136

Olivette, 138, 139
Open stage, 36, 37
Orchestra, 125
Orchestra pit, 125, 126
Outdoor theater, 42–43

Panel, 130
Pantomime, exercises in, 52, 55–56
Plano-convex spotlight, 139
Projection booth, 125
Projections, scenery, 133
Prompt book (prompt script), 93
Props
    dress, 136
    effects, 137
    hand, 106, 119, 136, 147
    personal, 106, 119, 136, 147
    rehearsal, 110
    scene, 136
    set, 136, 137
    trim, 136
Proscenium arch, 34, 125, 126, 134
Proscenium stage, 39, 41, 95, 124–127
Public domain, 4, 19

Reading rehearsal, 104–105, 117
Readers theater, 24–25
Rehearsals
    actors in, 115–120
    directors in, 99–115
    planning, 89, 102–104
    schedule, sample, 103
    types of, 104–114
Role, working on a, 71–83
Royalties, 3–4
Roscolene, 141
Run-through rehearsal, 110–112, 118–119

Scene-playing rehearsal, 108–110, 118
Scenery
    functions of, 128–129
    standard units, 129–133
Scoop, 138
Scoring a role, 59–60
Screen, 133, 136
Scrim, 131
Script analysis, 72–76
Sets, standard units, 133–136
Sound effects, 112–143
Stage areas, 95
Stage draperies (see Drapes)
Stage house, 124–126
Stages (see Theaters)
Stanislavski, Constantin, 56, 59
Striplights, 138

Teaser, 125, 126
Technical rehearsals, 112–113, 119
Theaters
    how to choose, 33–45
    improvising and adapting
    indoor
        cafeteria, 37–38
        classroom, 36
        extended proscenium, 41
        gymnasium, 39–40
        outdoor, 42–43
    portability of, 34–35
    types of, 42–43, 124–127
Theater-in-the-round, 36, 37, 39, 127
Tormenters (torms), 125, 126, 130
Thrust stage, 36, 38, 40, 127
Traps, 125, 126
Traveler, 125

Unit set, 136
U-shaped theater, 37
Upstaging, 92

Window flat, 129
Wing (scenery unit), 132, 136
Wing-and-border set, 136
Wings (stage location), 125, 126
Working script, 93–96

158